THE EMERGING POLICE STATE

RESISTING ILLEGITIMATE AUTHORITY

WILLIAM M. KUNSTLER

EDITED BY MICHAEL STEVEN SMITH
KARIN KUNSTLER GOLDMAN & SARAH KUNSTLER

INTRODUCTION BY MICHAEL RATNER

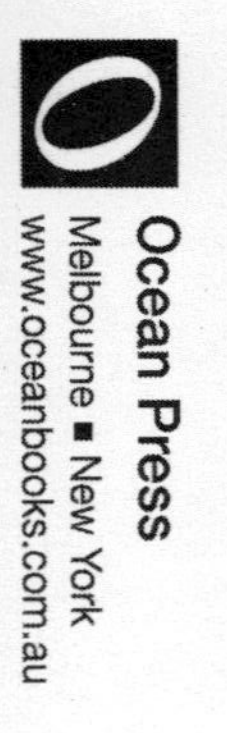

Cover design by ::maybe

ISBN 1-876175-79-6
Library of Congress Control No: 2003100601

First Printed in Australia 2004

Published by Ocean Press

Australia: GPO Box 3279, Melbourne, Victoria 3001, Australia
Fax: (61-3) 9329 5040 Tel: (61-3) 9326 4280
E-mail: info@oceanbooks.com.au

USA: PO Box 1186, Old Chelsea Stn.,
New York, NY 10113-1186, USA

Ocean Press Distributors:

United States and Canada: **Consortium Book Sales and Distribution**
Tel: 1-800-283-3572 www.cbsd.com

Australia and New Zealand: **Palgrave Macmillan**
E-mail: customer.service@macmillan.com.au

Britain and Europe: **Pluto Books**
E-mail: pluto@plutobooks.com

Cuba and Latin America: **Ocean Press**
E-mail: oceanhav@enet.cu

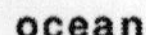

CONTENTS

DEDICATION AND ACKNOWLEDGMENTS iv

INTRODUCTION: THE OBLIGATION TO RESIST ILLEGITIMATE AUTHORITY
MICHAEL RATNER 1

WILLIAM MOSES KUNSTLER (1919–95)
MICHAEL STEVEN SMITH 7

1. Public Ethics and the Bill of Rights 15
2. The Origins of the U.S. Constitution 29
3. What Is Law? 38
4. The Outer Limits of Advocacy 44
5. On Violence 48
6. FBI-Transcribed Speech at Western Kentucky University 50
7. FBI-Transcribed Speech in Bowling Green, Kentucky 60
8. Summation for the Defense in the Chicago Seven Trial 63
9. FBI-Transcribed Speech in Jacksonville, Florida 75
10. FBI-Transcribed Speech in San José, California 79
11. Defending Flag Burning as Symbolic Speech 85
12. Concerning Free Speech for Racists and Totalitarians 90
13. Commemorating the 1970 Murder of Four Students 94
14. Devoting Yourself to Others 110
15. The Movement is Not Dead 114

AFTERWORD: BILL KUNSTLER, AN APPRECIATION
HON. GUSTIN L. REICHBACH 116

CONTRIBUTORS 121

DEDICATION

For death row prisoners Mumia Abu-Jamal, whose freedom always concerned Bill, and Ryan Matthews, falsely condemned as a teenager in Louisiana; for René González, Ramón Labañino, Fernando González, Gerardo Hernández and Antonio Guerrero, five Cubans who defended their country against U.S. protected terrorists and who are now in U.S. prisons for preventing deaths on the island; and Lynne Stewart, Bill's courageous colleague, indicted in the terrorist scare after 9/11 for vigorously representing her Muslim client.

ACKNOWLEDGMENTS

The editors wish to thank Gerald Lefcourt, Katey McGrath, Randy Credico, Michael Ratner, and Ben Elson for locating materials for the book, Terese Nehrbauer for typing and editing the manuscript, Sarah Plant for technical advice, Debby Smith for copy editing, and Margaret Ratner Kunstler for her acumen, encouragement and kindness.

INTRODUCTION

THE OBLIGATION TO RESIST ILLEGITIMATE AUTHORITY

MICHAEL RATNER

This book is a breath of fresh air. Reading Bill's speeches genuinely awed me. They made me optimistic about the fight to regain our lost liberty. His speeches are as prescient today as they were when he gave them. His words place our struggle for a more just world in a historical context of struggle, and should make us all understand the obligation to continue fighting.

Bill's words are truly inspiring and meaningful, not just with regard to the tumultuous period in which they were mostly written – the 1960s and 1970s, the height of the struggle for black civil rights and against the Vietnam War – but inspiring for today. His ideas are fresh and informed by his understanding of history. He connects the oppression present in the eras of Jesus and Socrates to the oppression underlying the trial of Sacco and Vanzetti; to the false prosecution of those who allegedly set the Reichstag fire; to the persecution of alleged communists in the United States; to the trial of the Chicago Seven, and the persecution of the Black Panthers. He sees oppression in the state killings at Attica, Jackson State, Kent State, Wounded Knee and the killing of Fred Hampton.

In challenging oppression, Bill never succumbed to pessimism. Rather, he viewed oppression within a context of struggle. His true heroes were those who stood up against oppression – whether it was colonists participating in the Boston Tea Party or Native Americans fighting to regain their ancestral lands. The fact that throughout history people have stood up against oppression is what called forth Bill's optimism and solidified his belief that all who care about liberty have an obligation to act. These speeches call all of us to take action and to see ourselves as links in a great and historical chain of struggle.

A number of speeches in this book illustrate how Bill's understanding of the role of law in the process of social struggle evolved. In his early days as a Westchester lawyer, and even when he represented Martin Luther King, Jr., he believed that law was a civilized means of settling disputes. He felt that whatever its shortcomings, the legal process was essentially a fair one and its defects could be remedied.

His thinking changed with the Chicago Seven conspiracy trial, which Bill called his personal Rubicon. After that trial, in which the trial judge sentenced Bill to more than four years for contempt of court, he no longer believed that law was a just system of settling disputes. Rather, from then on, law to him was a means of social control by the powers that be who were "determined, at all costs, to perpetuate themselves." Bill believed the entire legal system was villainous.

In one of his many great speeches, Bill analyzed trials including those of Jesus, Socrates, Kent State, the Harrisburg Eight, Dr. Spock and the man accused of setting the Reichstag fire. To Bill, these trials were not just about a society ridding itself of its critics and revolutionaries, they were also about demonization. They were about fabricating enemies and terrifying the citizenry. Trials such as these provided a means for the state to become more and more repressive. People tolerated this repression because they were afraid. Bill was fond of describing the Orwell character, Goldstein, in *1984*. As Bill said, Big Brother (the state) kept Goldstein alive as "an enemy of the state… to remind the people… that [Big Brother] was protecting them against this awful enemy, this fabricated enemy."

Bill's teaching regarding "fabricated enemies" is extremely relevant today. Today's fabricated enemies are Muslims, people of Arabic ethnicity and immigrants in general. The U.S. government has used the attacks of September 11, 2001, to keep us in a state of perpetual fear and has implicated entire communities as "enemies" to do so. It has frightened the population and terrified the country. Then, in the name of making us safer, the state has done exactly what Bill said a state always does – repress dissent, legislate draconian laws, curtail our freedom and use the law as a means of social and economic control. The citizenry are willing to accept these measures, as they did in Germany after the Reichstag fire, because they are fearful. As Bill said, because people were afraid, the "people tolerated the noose until it was too late to move." Bill believed that was happening in the 1960s and 1970s and he would certainly believe that is what is happening today.

Bill made a strong call for resistance to the repression he saw around him. He called for "resistance to illegitimate, immoral, indecent and unjust authority." He was willing to take risks himself, told people not to cooperate with the draft and told them to destroy the surveillance cameras photographing their demonstrations. Such resistance was swirling around him during this period. It ran the gamut from civil disobedience to burning draft records and even bombing the capital. Bill refused to condemn this resistance out of moral solidarity with the resisters. When students were called violent for their actions, Bill placed the blame squarely on the government and those seeking to hold back social progress. He asked who was com-mitting the real violence in the United States and answered that it was not the students and the radicals. *They* were not bombing Vietnam; *they* did not kill Martin Luther King, Jr. and Medgar Evers.

In the mid-1970s, Bill was accused of condoning the murders of John and Robert Kennedy. Bill answered that he had never condoned their murders, and was grieved by their deaths. Bill believed that their assassinations happened "because its [America's] leaders have plotted and used those means against others." He pointed out that the United States had engaged in invasions, brought death and destruction to hundreds of thousands of innocent people in Vietnam and taught a generation of Americans to murder. Bill's effort to connect violence in the United States with U.S. violence abroad was not popular. In fact, an attempt was made by a bar association to discipline him for these very ideas.

This unwillingness of a society to see the connection between the violence it practises against others, and the violence visited upon it, is highly relevant today. Shortly after the September 11 attacks, some brave critics sought to examine the reasons such violence might have occurred. They argued that one must understand the role of the United States, particularly in the Middle East, to truly get at the roots of September 11. They pointed to U.S. support for dictatorial regimes and its support for Israel in its inhuman policy toward the Palestinians. These critics were called traitors and practically drummed out of the country.

Bill would have been especially articulate regarding the draconian cutbacks in our civil rights that are now occurring under the guise of fighting terrorism. Ironically, some of Bill's speeches on resistance were preserved for us courtesy of the Federal Bureau of Investigation (FBI), our national political police force. The speeches were obtained through Sarah Kunstler's Freedom of Information Act request. The Freedom of Information Act was a victory of the 1960s. Today, an edict of Attorney General John Ashcroft has closed this window of democracy and obtaining these papers would be difficult, if not impossible.

Bill would have surely seen the current repression by Attorney General Ashcroft, Secretary of Defense Rumsfeld and others as the hallmark of a police state. He was particularly concerned with the whittling down of the fundamental protections of the Bill of Rights, particularly those embodied in the First, Fourth, Fifth and Sixth Amendments. He gave a wonderful talk about these rights and the government efforts in the 1960s and 1970s to eviscerate them. (See Chapter One: Public Ethics and the Bill of Rights).

Bill's comments about the importance of these protections are especially relevant today, during this time of resurging repression. We are facing the most sustained and deepest assault on liberty that we have ever seen. Bill would have been everywhere, rousing us all to fight on and oppose the government in every way we can. Bill would have been out there fighting to protect our First Amendment right to dissent and to do so free from government surveillance. He would have condemned the broadened FBI guidelines that allow spying on political and religious activists, the arrest of demonstrators all over the country, the surveillance programs to gather all kinds of information on everyone living in the United States, and the TIPS program asking us to report the "suspicious activities" of our neighbors, making spies of us all.

Bill would have been shocked by the wholesale violations of the Fourth Amendment, which was designed to protect us from illegal government searches and arrests. Under the Patriot Act, the government can now go to a secret court and wiretap people for purposes of prosecuting crimes; no longer is "probable cause" needed for such wiretaps. The warrant protections of the Fourth Amendment have been eviscerated. Normally, law enforcement officials need probable cause that one has committed a crime to effectuate an arrest and keep one in detention. That is no longer the case. People can now be detained indefinitely, without probable cause and without a trial. That is occurring to hundreds of people in Guantánamo, to "enemy combatant" U.S. citizens held in military brigs in the United States and to hundreds of noncitizens detained after September 11. The majority of these people never even get to test their detentions in a court.

Trials of those accused of "terrorism" are a mockery of any judicial system that wants to call itself fair and just. The Fifth Amendment requires due process of law. Bill was already condemning its loss and pointed to Supreme Court cases that said it was perfectly all right to have a lawyer and a trial that do not meet high standards, just so long as you have a trial. What would he have said today about the military commissions carried out without juries, rules of evidence, and with no appeal except to the president who designated the defendant for such a "trial" in the first place?

The Sixth Amendment guarantees the right to a lawyer and a jury trial for criminal defendants. Bill already thought that that amendment was "pretty well up in smoke." Today the situation is far worse. Lawyers defending alleged terrorists can be routinely wiretapped without the government getting any authority from any court, even a secret court. The government has denied lawyers to those in Guantánamo and enemy combatants held in the United States. The government has struck the Sixth Amendment from the constitution and so far the courts have willingly gone along.

Yet, despite this awful state of affairs, Bill would have been optimistic. He would have implored us to fight on, not to give up hope and to defend those the government has set its sights on. He would not have stepped out of the fray. He would have also understood that the battle for a just society would not be won in the courtroom, and that all of us have an obligation to resist – to resist illegitimate authority. As Bill so eloquently admonished: "The struggle to maintain human liberty and to resist oppression and tyranny is the perennial obligation of all who understand its necessity."

WILLIAM MOSES KUNSTLER (1919–95)

MICHAEL STEVEN SMITH

A month before he died, Bill Kunstler performed a stand-up routine at Caroline's Comedy Club in Manhattan. I wasn't surprised to see the announcement in the *New York Times*. He was entertaining and extremely funny. Recently, he had cracked up a bunch of us outside my office door with a terrific Groucho Marx imitation. His high spirits and irreverence, even about himself, rubbed off on people, making them feel good about themselves. Even though he was 76, he said he would never retire. Instead, he envisioned himself "checking out" while delivering a summation to a jury, sinking to the courtroom floor, clutching his notes.

One of Bill's favorite stories came out of the Chicago Seven trial. Someone had mailed him a vegetable substance, and he immediately called its receipt to the attention of Judge Julius Hoffman. "What are you telling me for?" remarked the obtuse judge (who the defendants referred to as Mr. Magoo). "Do something with it yourself."

"I assure you, Your Honor, that I will personally burn it tonight," Bill responded.

I remember a talk that Bill gave on the death penalty at the New York Marxist School. As he was leaving, a group of people gathered around him asking for his address. "Here is a get-out-of-jail-free card," he offered, producing several business cards from his wallet and handing them out.

I met Bill for the first time in 1966, when I was a law student at the University of Wisconsin. Although he was a generation older than I, we were radicalized at the same time. Hundreds of lawyers like myself, products of the 1960s, many in the National Lawyers Guild, strongly identified with and were constantly inspired by Bill. He spoke at the law school about government repression, using the metaphor of "silken threads" descending and strangling. The honorarium was $1,000, which I was happy to help get for him, and which went from his hands directly into the movement, as usual. I saw him some years later at the City Hall subway entrance. His hand came up from his pocket empty after fishing for a token. "Here," I said, offering him a token and putting it in the slot. "Now it is $1,001," he replied, as he walked through the turnstile.

On another occasion, Bill was at my office for a deposition. This time, he was the defendant. Michael O'Neill of Syracuse and I had the good fortune of defending him against a trumped-up legal malpractice action. Bill charmed the socks off the opposing attorney, a guy who had flown up with his associate from Washington, D.C., and who had paid a whole lot of money to have Bill's testimony videotaped.

The deposition, with Bill sitting at the end of the table on camera, lasted all day. The D.C. lawyer did not lay a glove on Bill, who remembered in detail events of eight years past. Then, the damnedest thing happened. When Bill got through cleaning the fellow's clock and the deposition ended, the D.C. guy – who had told us during the course of the hearing that he had earlier worked for the Federal Bureau of Prisons as the assistant to the director – got up from the conference table, leaned over, and hugged Bill. And you know, despite Bill's feelings about the Bureau of Prisons, he bore the D.C. guy no personal malice. He hugged him back. Indeed, during the course of the entire morning and afternoon of the deposition, when Bill was being sued for a telephone number that, if enforced, would have wiped him out, Bill had nothing but kind words to say about the plaintiff, and he sincerely meant it.

Incidentally, Bill had lost a letter he had written to the plaintiff. Had Bill been able to produce the letter, the plaintiff's bogus suit would have been shown to be groundless. But he could not find it. "Just say what you had written in it," I volunteered, figuring that any stick would do to beat a dog. But Bill would not do it, and then, as if to show that virtue is sometimes more than its own reward, several weeks later Bill found the exculpatory letter.

Bill's 75th birthday party at Gus's Place, his favorite Village restaurant, was so full of laughs that I was left reeling. He talked about his early childhood in Harlem and told of being a mischievous troublemaker, a "real pisser," "Peck's bad boy," as he put it. Truly, as Milton wrote, "Childhood shows the man, as morning shows the day."

Bill went on to relate a story about himself. He had been representing the mobster John Gotti (on the issue of whether Gotti had the right to choose his own lawyer), and he was invited out to dinner with Gotti and his crowd. Bill was asked at the restaurant if he would please make a toast. He rose from the table, glass in hand, and declared, "Here's to crime." The entire gathering sat stone silent staring at him. Bill then exited. After he left, they all fell out.

Bill first got involved in the civil rights movement by representing freedom fighters from the North who helped desegregate interstate travel. He stayed committed to the black struggle for four decades until the end of his life, representing Martin Luther King, Jr., as his personal attorney for six years. He also represented Malcolm X's daughter. He had left a successful Westchester practise with his late brother, Michael, and eventually set up an office in the basement of his house on Gay Street in the Village, which he told me had been a stop on the Underground Railroad.

With characteristic courage, Bill confronted a Supreme Court judge, saying he was "a disgrace to the bench" because of a racist ruling he had made. The judge then lodged a formal complaint against Bill with the Character and Fitness Committee of the Bar, asking that Bill be "disciplined." Bill found himself in the courthouse in downtown Manhattan. The room was packed with his supporters. Bill spoke about his beliefs and his life: DeWitt Clinton High School, Yale, Phi Beta Kappa, Army Major, World War II in the Pacific, Bronze Star, Columbia Law School (Stone Scholar).

Morton Stavis, Bill's good friend and president of the Center for Constitutional Rights (Bill was a vice-president, founder and volunteer attorney), elicited more of the details on Bill's accomplishments. Then Bill concluded with speaking about his representation of the Attica brothers, Fred Hampton, Assata Shakur, the Harlem Six and Larry Davis. He spoke of his friendship with Malcolm X, whom he admired immensely. The effect of Bill's testimony on me and everyone else in that room was powerful and deeply moving. "We are in the presence of a great and fine American," I thought at the time. The panel must have thought similarly, because when their "disciplinary" decision came down, it hardly amounted to a slap on the wrist.

Bill Kunstler's legal accomplishments in the defense of African Americans and democratic rights are of great historical significance. Bill undertook cases, as he would say, to make a point and educate people. Fees were not important to him. Often, he did not charge any fee at all, and when he did, he never kept very good track of it. On wealth, he said, "Just get enough to live on. Animals that overeat die." On his career of litigating, he said in a 1993 interview, "Over all, I never counted, but my lifetime batting average is probably better than Willie Mays." His victories included:

- Trial Counsel, *Adam Clayton Powell v. McCormack* (1966 reinstatement to Congress case)
- Trial Counsel, *Hobson v. Hansen* (1966 Washington, D.C., school desegregation case)

- Trial Counsel, *Stokely Carmichael v. Allen* (1967 invalidation of Georgia Insurrection Statute)
- Trial Counsel, *McSurley v. Ratliff* (1968 invalidation of Kentucky Sedition Statute)
- Trial Counsel, *U.S. v. Berrigan* (1968 defense of Catholic antiwar activists accused of destroying draft records at Catonsville, Maryland)
- Trial Counsel, *U.S. v. Dellinger* (1969–70 Chicago Eight conspiracy case)*
- Trial Counsel, *U.S. v. Dennis Banks and Russell Means* (defense of American Indian Movement leaders accused of a number of crimes in the takeover of Wounded Knee, South Dakota, in 1973)
- Trial Counsel, *U.S. v. Sinclair* (1971 invalidation of government's claim of unrestricted wiretapping powers)
- Trial Counsel, *U.S. v. Butler and Rabat* and Appellate Counsel, *U.S. v. Leonard Peltier* (defense of American Indian Movement members on charges stemming from 1975 shootout on Pine Ridge Reservation, resulting in the deaths of one Native American and two FBI agents)
- Appellate Counsel, *Texas v. Johnson and Eichmann et al.* (1989 and 1990 Supreme Court arguments in flag-burning cases)

Foreign empires, like people, don't change with age. My Aunt Lil used to say, "As people grow older, they don't change, they just

*THE CHICAGO EIGHT BECAME KNOWN AS THE CHICAGO SEVEN AFTER BLACK PANTHER LEADER BOBBY SEALE'S CASE WAS SEVERED FROM THE CASE OF THE ORIGINAL EIGHT. SEALE HAD RETAINED ATTORNEY CHARLES GARRY, WHO ASKED FOR A SHORT ADJOURNMENT DUE TO EMERGENCY SURGERY. PRESIDING JUDGE JULIUS KAUFMAN REFUSED GARRY'S ROUTINE REQUEST AND THEN REFUSED SEALE'S REQUEST TO REPRESENT HIMSELF. NONETHELESS, SEALE SPOKE UP AND WHEN HE PERSISTED IN ASSERTING HIS DEFENSE, JUDGE KAUFMAN HAD HIM GAGGED AND SHACKLED IN THE COURTROOM. THE SPECTACLE OF A BLACK MAN SO BOUND AT THE BAR OF JUSTICE CAUSED JUDGE HOFFMAN TO SEVER SEALE'S TRIAL FROM THAT OF THE OTHERS.

get more so." The U.S. empire became "more so" after its success in 1991 in overturning the Soviet Union and Eastern Europe, more precisely, in restoring private property relations in place of nationalized property, the last vestiges of the Russian Revolution. The U.S. empire is now referred to in the media, unashamedly, as "imperialist."

The swelling imperialist domination abroad was necessarily accompanied by a tightening of social control at home. Following the tragedy of 9/11, the USA Patriot Act was hastily pushed through a cowed and fearful Congress. Members voted on the 342-page bill, which was largely a compilation of past proposed legislation, that had failed because of its encroachments on civil liberties, without even reading it. The American Civil Liberties Union received phone calls from congressional aides afterwards asking what they had voted for. This was followed by the construction of the 170,000 person strong Department of Homeland Security. Shortly thereafter, the Terrorist Information Awareness Program was set up under the aegis of the Pentagon in order to establish a giant database on U.S. citizens. Bill Kunstler both anticipated and resisted these police state assaults on our liberties.

Possessed of a sonorous, compelling, bass voice, able to call up from memory references from art history, history, poetry and prose, Kunstler was one of the great speakers of his time. Like his contemporary, the magnificent orator Malcolm X, who Bill knew and greatly admired, Bill was widely sought after as a speaker and listened to, especially by young people.

With the modern media being what it is, and with Bill's expert use of it, he probably had more of an impact on more people in his time than Clarence Darrow had in his. Bill was featured on "Face the Nation," the "Today Show," "Good Morning America," "20/20," "60 Minutes," "Prime Time Live" and the "Donohue Show," to name a few. He was a guest on countless radio programs throughout the country. He was even a member of the Screen Actors Guild, playing the role of Jim Morrison's attorney in Oliver

Stone's *The Doors* and the role of the judge in Spike Lee's *Malcolm X*. Bill was also a consultant to Oliver Stone for *In the Spirit of Crazy Horse*. Bill wrote articles for dozens of law reviews and magazines. He also wrote 13 books. In 1941, his first book of poems came out, *Our Pleasant Vices*, which was followed by two others, *Trials and Tribulations* (1985) and *Hints and Allegations* (1994). He wrote two books on the technical aspects of legal practise, and even produced a bestseller (*The Minister and the Choir Singer* – 1964). Bill's book on the civil rights struggle of the 1960s, *Deep in My Heart*, is dedicated to several hundred fellow attorneys who went South for the struggle.

Bill had no funeral. He wasn't religious. Religion to him was superstition. Being part of a sect was too narrow and confining. The Jewish heretic who transcends Jewry belongs to a Jewish tradition. The historian Isaac Deutscher had a phrase for it, "the non-Jewish Jew." Bill was in line with the great heretics, rebels and revolutionaries of modern thought: Spinoza, Heine, Marx, Luxemburg, Trotsky and Freud. They all went beyond the boundaries of Jewry, finding it too narrow, archaic, constricting.

I do not wish to stretch the comparison. Bill was not so much a radical thinker as a man of action. But his intellectual understanding – and he was extremely well-educated – powered his activity. He had in common with these great thinkers the idea that for knowledge to be real it must be acted upon. As Marx observed: "Hitherto philosophers have only interpreted the world, the point now is to change it."

Like his intellectual predecessors, Bill saw reality in a state of flux, as dynamic and not static, and he was aware of the constantly changing and contradictory nature of society. Bill was essentially an optimist and shared with the great Jewish revolutionaries an optimistic belief in humanity and a belief in the solidarity of humankind.

At the end of the Civil War, when the guns were still crackling and the Union troops (many of them African American) marched in to take over the remaining Southern posts, a song was often on their lips:

> *John Brown's body lies a-moldering in the grave,*
> *John Brown's body lies a-moldering in the grave,*
> *John Brown's body lies a-moldering in the grave,*
> *But his truth goes marching on.*

So does Bill's.

CHAPTER ONE

PUBLIC ETHICS AND THE BILL OF RIGHTS

INTRODUCTORY NOTE

BY BRUCE JACKSON (PROFESSOR, UNIVERSITY OF BUFFALO)

Civil rights attorney William M. Kunstler was the speaker at the May 13, 1995, Buffalo School of Architecture and Planning Commencement (SUNY). The dean of that school, Bruno Freschi, thought it might do his students more good to hear someone talk about ethics than about the glories of design or planning.

Kunstler based much of his talk on 10 violations of the Bill of Rights he came across in that morning's *New York Times*. He spoke of racism, corruption, gay bashing by a member of Congress, violence and brutality.

I think of Kunstler, and that speech in particular, a good deal these days. I think of them when I read articles in the *New York Times* about teenagers locked in federal jails with no formal charges they might answer; Texas officials fighting to keep in state prison dozens of blacks from the town of Tulia they know are totally innocent; federal prisoners facing secret trials with no access to lawyers or their own families; the concentration camp for prisoners of war maintained by the U.S. government in a naval base in Cuba; a Pennsylvania senator saying it's okay to be gay but not to do it (is that like it's okay to be a Christian or a Jew but not okay to engage in any of the behaviors connected with those conditions?); protesters locked up by federal agents merely for standing with placards where President Bush might happen to see them; Attorney General Ashcroft and his minions secretly polishing Patriot II; Bush Administration officials insisting that criticism of them in a time of war is traitorous – and the same officials vowing a never-ending war against the world's evil, here and abroad.

William Kunstler was for many years the best-known civil rights attorney in the United States. He had, since he first represented Freedom Riders attempting to integrate interstate buses in Mississippi in 1962, been a central figure in nearly every major civil rights case. Because many of his early clients are now American heroes, it is easy to forget that at the time Kunstler represented them, most were American pariahs. He represented or worked with Martin Luther King, Jr., Lenny Bruce, Malcolm X, Phillip and Daniel Berrigan, H. Rap Brown, Stokely Carmichael, Adam Clayton Powell, the Chicago Seven, Jack Ruby, Attica prisoners, Black Panthers, Wounded Knee Indians and countless others.

Bill Kunstler was a warrior who elected to fight in the civil atmosphere of the courthouse rather than the streets. He had earned his choice: in World War II, he was awarded the Bronze Star and the Purple Heart. He saw corruption and ineptitude and laziness and malevolence in our government, but he adored the ideas of human rights underlying our system of government. He believed passionately in the Bill of Rights. Those amendments to the U.S. Constitution were, to him, a sacred text, and he was outraged and energized by attempts to dilute or abrogate the freedoms they guaranteed.

"Every generation has its time to struggle," Kunstler told those 1995 architecture graduates. "There are no green pastures."

This was one of the last public addresses William Kunstler gave. He died four months later, on September 4, 1995.

⌛ ⌛ ⌛

COMMENCEMENT REMARKS TO THE SCHOOL OF ARCHITECTURE AND PLANNING STATE UNIVERSITY OF NEW YORK AT BUFFALO, MAY 13, 1995.

There are two firsts for me here today. I haven't had one of these academic gowns on since I left the sacred precincts of New Haven and Yale University to join the U.S. Army in 1941. Secondly, I haven't been called honorable, I think, by anybody in this country at least, for the last 40 years. Though it is unpleasant to wear this robe in this heat and pleasant to be called honorable, neither will last longer than today, believe me. Tomorrow I will be back in contempt somewhere going into one jail or another, where I always get a urological check-up and dental care. The reason I have kept all of my teeth all these years has been that every good county jail in America has a relatively decent dental program.

When Bruno Freschi called me up and asked me what I was going to talk about, he suggested a subject, and because of his strong Canadian voice, I thought he was asking me to speak about "sex." It actually was "ethics." But I kept hearing sex, and I wrote on a pad to my partner, "The idiot wants me to talk about sex." And he wrote back, "What do architectural and planning students have to do with sex?" All we could think of was erections. But then it came through loud and clear that what he was saying was ethics and not sex. So I crossed "sex" off the pad, I put "ethics" down, my partner lost interest completely, and I prepared whatever I'm going to say today.

Ethics are important, although they don't exist very much in the United States – or maybe anywhere for that matter. On the way up on the plane, I had the *New York Times* on my lap, and I thought I would look and see how ethics were faring in the United States. I found 10 items:

One was a squib that a district attorney in Rockland County had pled guilty earlier in the week to income tax evasion and fraud.

The second was that welfare recipients had entered into a conspiracy with the welfare people who signed the checks. They were receiving checks for a quarter of a million dollars in some instances and the total defrauding of the welfare system of the City of New York was $2.2 million.

The third item was a New York City police officer pleading guilty to three counts of cocaine possession.

The fourth was the execution last night of a hopelessly insane man in Alabama by electrocution.

The fifth was a New Orleans police officer, a woman, alleged to have killed three people in a Vietnamese restaurant in that city while two of them were on their knees begging for mercy.

The sixth was a Jersey City police officer suspended for killing a man in custody by beating him about the head so seriously he went into a coma and died yesterday.

The seventh was a divorce lawyer who had hired a thug to break the leg of his opponent, another divorce lawyer, in a contested divorce proceeding.

The eighth was Kay Wall, who had been appointed by Governor John Rowland of Connecticut to the Board of Education of the state – which Governor Rowland had turned into all white now from three blacks, one Hispanic and one white. But she was forced to disclaim her appointment because she had made an unfortunate remark that people would love her if she were black, had black hair, was 20 pounds heavier and came from the ghetto of Hartford. Because of that remark, she withdrew her nomination.

The ninth was a congressman referring to gay people as "homos."

And the tenth was another congressman referring to Waco – that unfortunate tragedy at Waco, Texas, two years ago – as a plot of Bill Clinton, and referring to the federal officers involved as "thugs in jack boots."

These 10, in one paper only. The word "ethics" apparently has very little meaning in the body politic.

Bruce Jackson referred me to a poem by John Berryman called "World Telegram," where he read in that newspaper (long out of print but which I used to read as a boy and young man) all of the terrible things that had happened on May 13, 1939. This is the final stanza of that poem:

> *News of one day, one afternoon, one time.*
> *If it were possible to take these things*
> *Quite seriously, I believe they might*
> *Curry disorder in the strongest brain,*
> *Immobilize the most resilient will,*
> *Stop trains, break up the city's food supply,*
> *And perfectly demoralize the nation.*

He was doing in 1939 what I am doing here today. Perhaps the best way to describe this breakdown of ethical concepts in this country (except in rare and isolated places – like the University of Buffalo) is a history of the attempts to establish some form of ethos in this country.

As you know, the American Revolution was not a revolution engineered by poor people or by people who sold rats for a penny a pound down on the Long Wharf in Boston. It was engineered by the wealthy who wanted to transfer the power of wealth from London to New York, Philadelphia and Boston. The people who *fought* it were those people who sold rats on the Long Wharf – the tinsmiths, the blacksmiths and so on. But those who gained the most from it were the wealthy, the slave owners.

They met in Philadelphia in 1787. They met at what's called Independence Hall, designed by a very famous lawyer, Andrew

Hamilton, who defended John Peter Zenger in that famous freedom of speech trial in 1735 in New York. They blacked out the windows with paint, so that no one would know they were going to violate their orders from those who sent them there by writing a new constitution and not reforming the Articles of Confederation, which was why they had been sent to Philadelphia. They were so afraid that people would find out what they were doing that they had Benjamin Franklin followed home every night and then followed from his lodgings to Independence Hall, because old Ben liked to tip a glass or two at the local tavern and they were afraid that he would give away the story before it was ready to be given away. They worked all summer and they evolved this document.

The document is fine. It sets up a tripartite form of government, and so on, but it says nothing about human rights whatsoever. And while they were talking about the supremacy clause in that document, somebody stood up and said, "How about a Bill of Rights?" This man was George Mason of Virginia. They voted on it. They voted 12 to one *against* a Bill of Rights. The only one that didn't vote against it was, strangely enough, [from] North Carolina. I guess those delegates from North Carolina would be very surprised to see that the man who sits in the U.S. Senate from that state today is Jesse Helms. They voted again. Again, 12 to one against a Bill of Rights.

And so, Mason left the convention, joined by John Randolph of Virginia and Elbridge Gerry of Massachusetts. The Constitution went out for ratification and they were so afraid that it would not be ratified that they made a two-thirds vote the ratification number, rather than unanimous. Five states immediately ratified – Georgia and Connecticut among them. But the big states of Virginia, New York and Massachusetts did not ratify immediately. In fact, as you know, the Federalist Papers were created by Hamilton, and Jay and Madison to try to sell the Constitution to the New York ratifying convention. Finally, Massachusetts – meeting in the Long Wharf in Boston and led by Elbridge Gerry – had an idea:

Massachusetts will ratify if you agree to have a Bill of Rights in the first Congress. There was agreement on that score and the three big states voted narrowly – three votes in New York and 10 in Virginia – and the Constitution became law.

There was an election, George Washington and John Adams were elected president and vice-president, and a Congress was elected. It met in Federal Hall (still standing in New York) in 1791 and there was a vote on a Bill of Rights. After thrashing it out for months, they finally got a Bill of Rights.

The Senate voted that it should not be binding on the states; the House voted that it *should* be binding on the states. The Senate won. (It took 600,000 lives between 1861 and 1865 to begin to make the Bill of Rights binding on the states.) It went out for ratification. Virginia ratified on December 15 of that year, and that became the anniversary year of the Bill of Rights.

It had 12 amendments. The first two were meaningless for present purposes; they were never voted in. They had to do with salaries for representatives and senators. You can see what was on their mind with reference to what came first. The Third – Freedom of Speech – became the First, and so on.

And this great ideal of the revolution, theoretically at least, became the Bill of Rights. We were the first nation on Earth to have crystallized human rights in a document that was binding at least on the federal government.

And yet, over the years it has been demolished, amendment by amendment by amendment. One after the other, you've had these terrible onslaughts, until today, the Contract With America – as you know the lunatics are running the asylum these days – the Contract With America takes out of the Bill of Rights the Fourth Amendment entirely. It consecrates all searches and seizures, whether there is or isn't a warrant, with the phrase, "if the constable believes that he or she was acting constitutionally." That obviates the application of the Fourth Amendment.

The Fifth Amendment with its due process of law: this

execution in Alabama yesterday of an insane man who did not even know he was being executed will show you how far the inroads go into the Fifth Amendment. You also know that they are executing 15 and 16 year olds and they are going to work on 14 year olds very shortly. We have become the charnel house of the Western world with reference to executions; the next closest to us is the Republic of South Africa. We are the only nation in the Western world to have capital punishment today. All of Western Europe has abolished it.

On the Sixth Amendment: we have taken lawyers away from their clients. Just witness John Gotti losing his lawyer, Bruce Cutler, on the eve of trial. We've utilized all sorts of devices to neutralize lawyers across the country, such as contempt citations and Rule 11 of the Federal Rules of Civil Procedure, which gives them the right to penalize lawyers, fine them, if some judge says the civil rights action you brought should not have been brought. I stand before you, the recipient of a $125,000 fine; the head of the NAACP legal defense fund, $40,000; the Christic Institute, a Roman Catholic civil rights legal and educational foundation – $1 million and out of business today.

I could go through all the amendments, one by one, and you would see how the First has been whittled down. Doctors, for example, are not permitted to tell patients who are before them of the option of abortion.

The Second Amendment is very lively, of course. The only ones who subscribe to it are members of the National Rifle Association. So, it is of small importance to us, except they only read the gun part of it – "all citizens shall be entitled to bear arms" – and they don't read at all the part saying those citizens should be in "a well-regulated militia." But that's not one of the amendments of the Bill of Rights that gives any meaning today to us.

The Third doesn't either. That's about quartering troops in private homes. I don't think any of you have troops quartered in private homes, unless it be your sons and daughters occasionally home from the post.

The Fourth Amendment was so vital to the colonists, because, you will remember, the King of England issued what were called writs of assistance – open-ended search warrants. They lasted as long as the king lived, and all the constable had to do was fill in the name. There was a famous case in Boston in the 1760s where James Otis, a fiery lawyer, defended 68 ministers to try to end writs of assistance. John Adams was a young lawyer in that courtroom, and when he heard Otis address the court, he said, "Then and there was the child 'independence' born in that courtroom." In any event, it was so important to them, they enacted the Fourth Amendment: no unreasonable searches and seizures. But now, it has been dribbled away, bit by bit.

The Fifth Amendment, I've already mentioned – due process.

The Sixth Amendment, right to counsel. I've already hinted at it, and this is not a law school class, so we don't have to go into all the details.

The Seventh doesn't mean anything to you. It has to do with juries and civil trials.

The Eighth is the amendment that talks about unreasonable penalties, bail and so on. We've completely eliminated that. Our penalties are draconian, from the death penalty to sentences of life imprisonment for possession of cocaine, for example, and the famous "three strikes and you're out" concept of the Contract With America. And bail has gone out the window. We have a new statute from 1984, one of Reagan's little droppings, that says essentially that the judge can deny you bail in bailable cases if the judge comes to the conclusion you are a risk to flee or you are essentially a danger to the community. But it is not decided on "beyond a reasonable doubt" or even on "probable cause." The statute says "clear and convincing evidence" and no one knows quite what that means.

We also have anonymous juries now, as you know – that would probably come under the Fifth Amendment or the Sixth Amendment – where the jurors have numbers instead of names. I tried a case in New York some years ago where juror 318 took the stand to be questioned, a white woman. My co-counsel leaned over to me and said, "Bill, is 318 a Jewish name?" Because you cannot tell anything except from physical characteristics of the identity of the jurors, whether they are of Italian, French, German extraction, Scandinavian, or what have you. Because you don't have the names.

I also throw into the Bill of Rights the Thirteenth, Fourteenth and Fifteenth Amendments, which are the great Civil War amendments. The attacks on affirmative action and so on are gradually destroying them as well.

We've come to the point, I guess, where we fear so much – crime in the streets, bombings, domestic terrorism and the like – that we are virtually willing to countenance giving up of rights because we think it will safeguard us in our daily lives, particularly in the urban centers of this country. We are succumbing, in a way, and I don't make the analogy too close, to what the German people did when the Third Reich began to plant its foot on human rights in Germany. It was better to have a strong man, it was better to curtail rights, to be safe from the Bolsheviks, to be safe from the Versailles Treaty, and so on. And they gave in to that fear, and fear is the most dangerous quotient in any community, democratic or otherwise. Once fear takes root, then people will say, "What does it matter really if he didn't get his Fifth, or Fourth, or Sixth or Eighth Amendment rights? That doesn't affect me. I'm not on trial for anything; I'm not in jail. What does it matter? That's the question Pastor Niemöller faced, when he said, "First they came for the Jews and I did not raise my voice, and then they came for me."

It's a hard question. Politicians pander to that fear. They talk about getting tough on crime, more executions, more prisons, prisons that would put the Marquis de Sade to shame. They thrive and get reelected on that score and the public duly applauds: "We've got a man, a woman in there who's tough on crime, ergo, let's follow whatever he or she says. Let's put the elected stamp of approval on the trampling of the Bill of Rights."

Jefferson warned against this when he said if anyone really starts to trample on the Bill of Rights, we ought to throw over the traces once more. Not quite his language, but the gist of it was there. He also said "I tremble for my country when I think that God is just." No sooner had the ink dried on the Bill of Rights when John Adams became president, succeeding George Washington. Then we had the Alien and Sedition Laws, as evil a set of statutes against civil rights and human rights as [has] ever been enacted in this country. President Lincoln suspended the writ of habeas corpus. The know-nothings take control from time to time. All sorts of things are done that show how weak and fragile this Bill of Rights is.

Last night I watched Judge Ito cry on television when he attended an anniversary meeting of the time when Japanese American citizens of this country were snatched from their homes and put in concentration camps; their property confiscated for the sole reason that they were Nisei, American citizens of Japanese ancestry – and that was countenanced by a supine Supreme Court as being perfectly valid and constitutional. Slavery was countenanced by another supine Supreme Court as being perfectly constitutional. Segregation of the races after the Civil War was countenanced as being perfectly constitutional. So we have these terrible lapses, because the ethics, the ethos, somehow vanishes in the exigencies of the moment, the perceived exigencies of the moment.

Every generation has its time to struggle. There are no green pastures.

Herman Melville wrote a book called *Moby Dick*. I was in the Attica yard on September 12, 1971, just 30 miles from here, sitting with an old client, Sam Melville, who was to have his head blown off the next morning with double-0 buckshot when the troopers moved in and killed 39 people, including guards as well as inmates. I said, "Sam, where'd you get the name Melville?"

He said, "I got the name Melville because I took it. My real name is not Melville, but I was so impressed by what he was saying in *Moby Dick* that I took that name."

"So," I said, "what about *Moby Dick*? It's just a whale story." I remember seeing a movie where Ahab was not Gregory Peck – that's your generation – but John Barrymore played the first Ahab in the first motion picture "Moby Dick." And I said, "It's just a whale story."

He said, "No, it's not, Bill. The white whale is evil that swims on unconquering and unconquerable. Everybody dies on the *Pequod*. The *Pequod* is smashed to smithereens by the whale. Ahab is lashed by the harpoon lanyard to the whale's back and is drowned, the men in the longboat are destroyed, but one man goes back to sea. You can remember his name: it was Ishmael." And that's how the book essentially ends, Ishmael goes back to sea. No matter how bad the situation gets, there is always someone who goes back to sea. As long as that continues and there are those people, and it's not the majority, believe me.

We sit here today in the comparative freedom of this institution and, yes, I'll say this country for the moment (though I don't believe it, too much), but I will say it, because of better men and women than we who went down in the dust somewhere in the line. They died or rotted in prisons, were expatriated, but they kept going. They were the Ishmaels of their time and our time.

This is not meant to be a speech of cynicism or to tell you how pessimistically I see the world. I've never seen it that way. I've spent over 50 years practising this so-called profession in one state or another. I just came here from Minnesota where Qubilah Shabazz was finally set free from her ordeal in Minneapolis, and next week I go somewhere else. And I am hopeful that there always will be those Ishmaels. Those are the people I really talk to and really look for, those who are like the David of Michelangelo's statue (which you have in the Delaware Park here). Michelangelo's *David* is a good example for all of you. This is the only representation in art of David before he kills Goliath. All the rest – Donatello's bronze, the paintings – show him holding up the severed head of Goliath, as Goliath leads the Philistines down the hills of Galilee toward the Israelites. Michelangelo is saying, across these four centuries, that every person's life has a moment when you are thinking of doing something that will jeopardize yourself. And if you don't do it, no one will be the wiser that you even thought of it. So, it's easy to get out of it. And that's what David is doing right there. He's got the rock in the right hand, the sling over the left shoulder, and he's saying like Prufrock, "Do I dare, do I dare?"

I hope many of you, or at least a significant few, will dare when the time comes, if it hasn't come already.

I'd like to close with a poem I have always loved by Arthur Hugh Clough. Arthur Hugh Clough was a strange individual. I think he's really a near first-rank English poet. He died just after the Battle of Bull Run. He had been going to school in the United States, and then he returned to England. He also confronted the Church of England. He didn't like its policies, he was a rebel. He fought all of his life and it caused him a lot of trouble. He died young, in his early forties. He died after witnessing, at least through the press, the slaughter at Bull Run #1, and after being rebuffed by the Church of England for his views against it. In 1861, just before he died, he wrote the following poem which I think symbolizes how I feel – it does it in verse – but it says essentially what I want to say to all of you in this moment I have up here at this rostrum.

Say not the struggle naught availeth,
The labor and the wounds are vain,
The enemy faints not, nor faileth,
And as things have been they remain.

If hopes were dupes, fears may be liars;
It may be, in yon smoke concealed,
Your comrades chase e'en now the fliers,
And but for you, possess the field.

For while the tired waves, vainly breaking,
Seem here no painful inch to gain,
Far back, through creeks and inlets making,
Comes silent, flooding in, the main.

And not by eastern windows only,
When daylight comes, comes in the light,
In front, the sun climbs slow, how slowly,
But westward, look, the land is bright.

Thank you.

CHAPTER TWO

THE ORIGINS OF THE U.S. CONSTITUTION

WILLIAM KUNSTLER'S EXPLICATION OF THE ORIGINS OF THE U.S. CONSTITUTION IS FROM A COMMUNITY TELEVISION INTERVIEW IN NEW YORK CITY ON OCTOBER 23, 1990.

PAPER TIGER TELEVISION: The first Constitution was signed on September 17, 1787. Who signed it? Fifty-five white men. Fifteen were slave owners. The four delegates from South Carolina owned 569 slaves between them. Thirty-four of the delegates were lawyers. Forty held government bonds. Half of the delegates had money loaned at interest. Who wasn't invited? Women, blacks, Native Americans, indentured servants and white men who didn't own any land at all. White men who didn't own enough land to qualify to vote in their state, that is, at least 87 percent of the population, weren't represented.

WILLIAM KUNSTLER: The Constitution was not originally supposed to have been written at all because the delegates were sent there for another purpose. They were to modify the Articles of Confederation so many were dissatisfied with since the articles were formulated some six or seven years earlier. The reason they didn't like the Articles of Confederation was that it made each state a sovereign country, to put it mildly, and [New] Jersey could block the goods from New York or put tariffs on and prevent goods going to Philadelphia and so on. So the money interests in the country were very disturbed because the articles were making commerce much too uneconomical for those who held the money interests in... the various states. So they sent their delegates to Philadelphia, delegates who were told to formulate new Articles of Confederation making commerce easier. But when the delegates got there, they abandoned all of that and they decided to create a new Constitution, a new Article of Confederation, to call it a Constitution, and to make it a country with a strong central government and eliminate the trade barriers as well. That's why there is a commerce clause in the Constitution.

And the people that went there were hardly representative of the rest of the country. And they were so secretive about what they were doing that they had people following Benjamin Franklin, who was a loud mouth, in order to keep him from spilling the goods at some local tavern about what was really going on with that constitution.

A great many of the aristocrats didn't attend, such as Thomas Jefferson, whom you might expect to find there. George Washington was sort of the chairman of the board during the writing. But the writing was done mainly by five or six people. And these five or six people – Hamilton, Madison, Jay and so on, designed a strong central government with a strong hinge on keeping the economic commerce flowing in the country. But the document that they created was one of so many compromises, between equality and slavery, for example, that it essentially had the seeds of its own destruction written into it.

For example, three-fifths of all black slaves were to be counted in the southern states for representation in Congress by members of the House of Representatives. That meant that each black was three-fifths of a human being. And that they would be counted even though they had no vote whatsoever and no role in government, so that the South could get more representatives in Congress than the North. Because they could count not only the whites but the slaves as well, but only three-fifths of the slaves. That was the compromise that the Northerners achieved. It also had no mention, of course, of women and women were no part of the Constitution, there were 55 men and the Constitution did not give them universal suffrage whatsoever. That wasn't to come for more than a century and a half in the future. It also did not end the slave trade. It kept slavery going as an institution and perpetuated the slave trade for another 20 years. It wasn't to end until 1808. And of course it did nothing about abolishing slavery at all. That took one million lives between 1861 and 1865 to accomplish that job. It did not guarantee anything to indentured servants who were in essence slaves as well, except that they received some sort of wage but couldn't move freely from their jobs because that was the price of passage across the Atlantic. And it did nothing for the Indian nations whatsoever. It mentioned the Indian tribes and nations, but gave them nothing whatsoever out of the Constitution. It was a white man's creation, a white man's document.

But there were people there at that convention, like George Mason for example, who did have some feeling for human rights. And therefore the idea of a Bill of Rights was born. The idea that after the Constitution, which does nothing except establish a government of course, it [then] has a number of articles establishing an executive branch, a legislative branch, a judicial branch, picking up the debts of the old Articles of Confederation and carrying them into the future and so on. But it said nothing about freedom of speech, freedom of worship, nothing about unreasonable searches and seizures, due process of law, the right to jury trial and all the rest that was so important for the Declaration of Independence.

And so the agreement was made that the Constitution would not be enacted, would not even be promulgated unless there was an absolute assurance that it would be followed by a Bill of Rights.

And without that promise of a Bill of Rights, there would be no Constitution. As it was, the Constitution barely got through. In many states it was by one or two votes that the Constitution was adopted and it took the Federalist Papers to get it through New York when Madison and Jay and Hamilton tried to convince the legislature – it was the legislatures of the different states, not the people in general, who would either reject or accept the Constitution. And the Federalist Papers were designed to convince New York, or its legislature, that it ought to adopt the Constitution. It got through in New York by just a couple of votes. The majority was very slim. And only by the dint of the intellectual prowess of these three men, and the Federalist Papers, which were all signed *publicus* but written by three different people when you go through them – so many by Jay, so many by Hamilton and so many by Madison. New York finally adopted the Constitution, as did eventually all of the states. And when the ninth state had adopted the Constitution, I think that was Connecticut, then the Constitution was declared in force. A number of states didn't sign until later and didn't adopt it until later but it became effective when they had the nine states having adopted it.

Then the question of the Bill of Rights. And the Bill of Rights, which was originally 13 amendments, or 12 amendments, was then whittled down to 10. And the only ones that were really significant in the human rights area were the First – freedom of speech, religion, the press, the right to assemble for redress of grievances; the Fourth, which had to do with unreasonable searches and seizures, and prohibiting them; the Fifth, which talked about due process of law; the Sixth, which guaranteed right to trial by jury in criminal cases or right to counsel of your choice; and the Eighth, which said that you could not have unreasonable bail or cruel and unusual punishment. They were the key amendments in those first 10 amendments to the Constitution. They were powerful amendments.

But since their adoption, they have been whittled down

considerably and in recent years that whittling process has accelerated. The First Amendment guaranteed, of course, freedom of the press, which meant of course, in modern days, freedom of cinema as well. And yet today we have films which the government doesn't like, like films about acid rain, being prohibited from getting the requisite export licenses to make them commercially profitable to export throughout the world.

The Fourth Amendment said no unreasonable searches and seizures. And now we have a situation where if the policeman who breaks into your home does so in good faith, then that's perfectly all right. And we have the anomaly of a policeman with a warrant for 202 South Washington Street breaking into 200 South Washington Street, by mistake, thinking 200 was 202, finding some drugs therein, and then the courts saying you can't suppress that even though he broke into the wrong home, because in good faith he thought he was going into the right place. Therefore the poor devil in 200 who had some drugs lying around and was caught on a warrant for someone living in 202, was convicted and could not set aside the verdict or suppress that evidence.

The Fifth Amendment, which was due process of law, has been virtually ripped apart by so many enactments of the Supreme Court. The question of due process now has been virtually eliminated by so many aspects that the court has legitimized. Due process now, for example, means that a defendant may be brought into a court, given the lawyer he doesn't want because he can't afford one, for example, and be convicted on that with that lawyer's aid or lack of aid and the Supreme Court will say that's perfectly all right even though you didn't want him, you had a lawyer, and we don't guarantee a perfect trial, only a trial.

On the Sixth Amendment with the right to counsel, you are not allowed, if you are poor, to have your counsel of choice just because the state pays for [them]. We now have anonymous juries. The Sixth Amendment guarantees the right of trial by jury. Now we have faceless, anonymous jurors sanctioned by the Supreme

Court. We even have in one tribunal, anonymous witnesses whose identities, like the jurors, are kept from the parties. So the Sixth Amendment is pretty well up in smoke as well.

We have under the Eighth Amendment, which guarantees bail, reasonable bail in almost every case, we now have preventive detention, which means essentially that you can be detained in jail prior to trial simply because some judge says you are too dangerous to let out, even though you haven't been convicted of any crime. And we have in the case of Hartford, Connecticut, ... 16 people desiring independence for the island of Puerto Rico, two of whom have been kept in jail now into their third year and nine of whom were kept for a year and a half, on the basis of preventive detention, which the Supreme Court has just sustained.

So the Bill of Rights is gradually being eroded under that Eighth Amendment with reasonable bail being required, we now have of course exorbitant bail, $1 million, $2 million, mainly for radicals who are caught up in the toils of the law. And talking about cruel and unusual punishment, we have the death penalty, now being brought to life after a brief hiatus, being brought to life in so many states that we have, I think, over 1,300 people on death row. We are executing now people who are juveniles, we are executing women, we are executing so many people in the minority areas, so many more blacks than whites, for example. And as you know, the Supreme Court has just ruled not that blacks are three-fifths of persons anymore, they are one-fifth of white persons because even though the statistics showed that [with] blacks who were victims, the perpetrators or killers of blacks were 80 percent less likely to receive the death penalty than when the victim was a white. That means that if a white was murdered, that life had four-fifths more value than the life of a black or a Latino or an Oriental or an American Indian. So we have that aspect of the Supreme Court and the right to privacy... which is so important to our lives, probably one of the most important rights is the right to privacy under the Bill of Rights. We now know that gay and lesbian people don't fit within that category and the Supreme Court has sustained sodomy statutes in Georgia, and that means everywhere else in the United States, against consenting adults who are gay and does that on the grounds that essentially there is no right of privacy for certain elements of the population.

So our Bill of Rights is vanishing bit by bit inexorably and the Constitution is, I guess, what Karl Marx once said about the 18th Brumaire of Louis Napoleon that he was asked to appraise, he read it and said, "This has glowing phrases, marvelous hyperbole." He says, "But I do not think it will be applied to all the people."

And that's essentially what the American Constitution is. It is something that is not applied to all the people. It is applied, in essence, to corporate interests, and as many people know, the great Fourteenth Amendment that came in after the Bill of Rights and after the Civil War, the amendment that guarantees equal protection among all peoples, that amendment has been the most fruitful help to the corporate structure in America because corporations banged out the idea before the Supreme Court that they were persons under the Fourteenth Amendment and therefore entitled to equal protection as well, which was used to kill all child labor laws, to end all restrictions on business, to end rampant capitalism and so on. You have the Fourteenth Amendment being used [for] just the opposite – not to help people, but to help corporate America in its march toward a rapacious capitalism that has had the effect of destroying many people both here and abroad.

"The Constitution is what the judges say it is," said one observer, and that's essentially what we have got. The judges are the arbitrators; the last arbitrators are the justices of the Supreme Court. And when you get a Supreme Court such as we have now, that is a conservative, right-wing court, then the Constitution will be interpreted in a conservative, right-wing way.

With reference to the Constitution, I wrote a sonnet about it to try to describe everything I have said here tonight, because the three-fifths of a man, all the other aspects are in this sonnet. And it reads as follows:

No glowing word or phrase could ever hide
That blacks were fractions of humanity,
A faceless, nameless, unseen, unheard tide
To those who swore they loved equality.

A million died to end hypocrisy
And bring the bondsman's era to an end.
But then the courts concocted a decree
That separation was the proper trend.

It took another 60 years before
The ancient paragraphs received full sway.
Today the promised freedom may once more
Have been suddenly interpreted away.

This document so filled with noble prose
Must seem to some a trifle comatose.

Then to show how it interprets away the rights of men and women, whether they be heterosexual or gay or lesbian or of different color or creed, I wrote one about the Supreme Court. And I wrote it before it became an eight-person court, when it was still nine, but fortunately we don't see a Bork or a Ginsburg there yet. This is the poem about the Supreme Court:

Each day precisely at the stroke of ten,
they stream in hierarchical array into their seats,
one woman and eight men,
to listen to the cases of the day.

For some the Constitution is as dead
As those who once spelled out its terms.
For others still there is no greater dread
Than playing Jeremiah to the worms.

The rights and liberties of yesteryear
That centuries have barely kept alive
Are preordained to fade and disappear
By a majority of only five.

Distracted by the carpet's mooted threads,
one hardly hears the falling of the heads.

And that essentially is what we have today. We have a Supreme Court interpreting a dying constitution, at the same time as Justice Burger celebrates the birthday of that corpse.

The rest of the story I guess will be written in the future. There is a struggle going on now as to who shall fill the ninth seat on the Supreme Court. The ninth seat is the important one. It is the swing seat, the seat vacated by Mr. Justice Powell, who was a conservative on one hand and liberal on the other. And while he was tough on so-called criminals, he at least kept the Constitution alive in the area of the Bill of Rights for people other than the law and order cases. And now the question is a new nominee [who] has replaced the two derelicts that were named by an aging president, (with, I guess, a crooked idea of what this country is all about), will now wonder whether Anthony Kennedy, if he becomes Justice Anthony Kennedy, will in some way restore the balance that existed when Justice Powell was there. The hope is that that will happen and that we will then begin a leftward trend – that is already very evident in Canada – and that we will then begin maybe to have the winds blow again from the right direction.

CHAPTER THREE

WHAT IS LAW?

REMARKS OF WILLIAM M. KUNSTLER IN ACCEPTING THE THURGOOD MARSHALL PRACTITIONER'S AWARD FROM THE NEW YORK STATE ASSOCIATION OF CRIMINAL DEFENSE LAWYERS ON JANUARY 27, 1994, AT THE GRAND HYATT HOTEL.

It is interesting, to me at least, that the awards given here tonight are to two Columbia Law School classmates who graduated from that illustrious institution almost a half-century ago. Since receiving our Ll.Bs, however, we have gone quite different ways, Jack [Weinstein] to a long tenure on the federal bench and I to a career as an attorney, on both the civil and criminal side, for the inside and outside agitators, dissidents, revolutionaries and other assorted pariahs of this, our common land. The difference in those routes is what I would like to discuss briefly, but hardly exhaustively, here tonight.

I am certain that the judge's outlook on the law is far different than my own. To him, I am sure, it is the considered response of a civilized society to the problem of reaching reasoned conclusions to disputes between the state and its citizens and among the latter themselves. Whatever its shortcomings, they are patently aberrational and remediable. To me, however, it is, in fundamental essence, nothing more than a method of control created by a socioeconomic system determined, at all costs, to perpetuate itself, by all and any means necessary, for as long as possible. Clarence Darrow put it even more expansively, 58 years ago, when he said "there is no such thing as justice — in or out of court."

In the beginning, I hardly felt this way. Through my years in the South with Dr. King, the Student Nonviolent Coordinating Committee, the Freedom Riders and the Congress of Racial Equality, among other groups and individuals I was privileged to represent, I was convinced that, whatever its transient defects, the legal institution was essentially a fair one. The Chicago Conspiracy Trial, which began on September 23, 1969, and ended some five months later, taught me that everything I learned in law school on this score, and earnestly believed, was totally false.

In that crucible on the 23rd floor of the Everett Dirksen Federal Building, I learned that the government would stop at nothing — including subordination of perjury, fabrication of documents, eavesdropping on attorney-client conferences and constant and vitriolic public denigration of both the defendants and their counsel — to carry the day; that the judge encouraged and facilitated this *modus operandi;* and that federal marshals were given free rein to bind and gag a black defendant and terrorize outraged spectators. In the face of this onslaught, we at the defense table learned the hard way that, if we were to have any chance whatsoever, we had to fight fire with fire. Accordingly, the courtroom became a battleground in which we tried to blunt every indecency with as much force and ingenuity as we could muster.

After Chicago, which was my personal Rubicon, many of my friends and foes alike tried to convince me that what took place in Judge Hoffman's courtroom was simply aberrational and that I should not regard the entire legal system as villainous. At first blush, I was willing to consider this appraisal but, as time went by, I came to understand that, in cases that worried or beset the Establishment, no gutter was too low. I also became conscious of the sad fact that prosecutors and law enforcement agents, on both the state and federal level, would resort to any dirty trick, no matter how heinous, to do their masters' bidding as well as satisfy their own ambitions.

Fortunately, the general public has, at long last, become increasingly aware of the proclivities of these public officials. Only recently, it was disclosed that a sizable number of New York state troopers had engaged in the transfer of impressions from fingerprint cards to various crime scenes in order to implicate innocent defendants, a method that FBI experts declared impossible last March in Judge Weinstein's own courtroom. Documents that tended to exonerate the alleged "Ivan the Terrible" were withheld by Assistant U.S. Attorneys, resulting in an initial death sentence in Israel. Here, in New York, in the cases growing out of the [1993] World Trade Center bombing, the government was finally forced to characterize highly prejudicial (and primarily untrue) leaks to the media by anonymous federal agents as "cowardice by anonymity" and "reprehensible." Just weeks ago, the prosecutor in the alleged Islamic conspiracy to blow up buildings, tunnels and bridges and murder public officials, in order to thwart a bail application, misled a federal judge into believing that he possessed highly incriminating tape-recorded conversations between two of the defendants when they did not exist.

I don't want to forget the judges, on both the federal and state level, who, in one way or another, regularly do the system's bidding. While some, including Judge Weinstein, occasionally try to ameliorate some of the most draconian aspects of the Establishment's law, all are enmeshed in its tentacles and daily carry out its dictates. Ironically, I was just denied admission to the Southern District's Criminal Justice Panel because it was determined by some anonymous Peer Review Group and Board of Judges that, despite almost 50 years of trial experience and CJA appointments throughout the country, the last being by Judge Weinstein in March of 1993, I was not considered to be among the "most qualified" applicants. The net effect is to give federal district judges the right to determine just who may – and who may not – represent indigent defendants, a clear blunting of the Sixth Amendment's guarantees.

Last month, a newspaper columnist bemoaned the fact that most lawyers had lost what he denominated their "passion" and had become merely high-priced tools of the economic system. Justifiably, lawyer bashing has become a staple on the late-night talk show circuit and in cocktail party repartee. We have reached the stage where a Rolex watch, a high-priced condo, a bulging portfolio and a late-model sports car have far more meaning to many practitioners than a burning desire to obtain bedrock justice for those segments of society to whom it is so systematically denied. We are allied, as "officers of the court," with the judges and the prosecutors, when we should be exclusively "officers of the client."

We steadfastly deny, or refuse to acknowledge, that the criminal justice system, insofar as blacks and other minority members are concerned, is merely a device to keep them at bay for as long as possible. In April of 1991, the New York State Judicial Commission on the Minorities filed its report with then Chief Judge Sol Wachtler. After four evidentiary hearings, public meetings in each county with a minority population of at least 10 percent, sessions with most of the state's judges and court administrators, and consultations with the leaders of various bar and community associations, the commission concluded: "There are two justice systems at work in the courts of New York State, one for whites, and a very different one for minorities and the poor." This "double-tiered justice" confirmed the sad fact that "inequality, disparate treatment and injustice remain the hallmarks of our state justice system."

The commission's report came and went without a significant ripple in the legal community. Both the governor and Judge Wachtler downgraded its conclusions and it has not had the slightest impact on the system in which all of us function on a daily basis. The tragic cancer of white racism continues to infect the police, the prosecutors, the courts, the prisons and the parole boards, while almost all of us either deny that it exists or turn our heads away from it. To the dominant lay population, panicked by the specter of violent crime and pandered to by ambitious politicians, the entire criminal justice system, from arresting officer to parole board member, represents its remaining margin of safety.

If the Constitution or the Bill of Rights threatens to cause any breach in the barricades, they must be disregarded. As the detective-protagonist in the television series, "NYPD Blue," informs one of his uneasy subordinates after using dramatic threats of violence to wring a confession from a suspect, "There was nothing unconstitutional about what I did because the man was clearly guilty." Our vaunted rights and liberties have become naught but inconvenient "technicalities" that stand foursquare in the way of neofrontier justice. "Good faith" excuses Fourth Amendment violations; "preventive detention" and draconian forfeitures and sentences negate the Eighth Amendment; the Sixth Amendment right to counsel is but a myth of the past, and due process has given way to the virtues of expediency.

It is ironic that I, a white man, should be given the Thurgood Marshall Practitioner's Award when we, as a nation, are busily engaged in dismantling his life's work. His antithesis now occupies his seat, while his words are relegated to the scrap heap of yesterday's oracles. Soon, I suspect, his name will grace a boulevard or a school, and he will join the shades of Dr. King, Malcolm X, Marcus Garvey and Frederick Douglass who were similarly honored once they were safely dead.

I do not want to be a discordant voice in what is, after all, an evening dedicated to honoring not only Jack and me, but all of you who must stand similarly reflected in our momentary hour of recognition. I accept the award in the name of all of my past clients, some of whom were physically or psychologically destroyed, some of whom suffered unjust convictions and are even now rotting in prisons around the country, and some of whom were viciously discredited by false innuendos of sexual misconduct, financial misdeeds or incompetence in office. It is they, and they alone, who have earned me this award and I receive it in their names and with the fervent hope that someday, somehow, we will find the hidden path that leads to what we have always outwardly prized but never attained – Equal Justice Under Law.

CHAPTER FOUR

THE OUTER LIMITS OF ADVOCACY

THIS SPEECH, DEALING WITH THE OBLIGATION OF CRIMINAL DEFENSE COUNSELS TO THEIR CLIENTS, WAS WRITTEN CIRCA 1970 AND FOUND AMONG KUNSTLER'S PAPERS. IT IS NOT KNOWN WHERE OR WHETHER IT WAS DELIVERED.

For generations, criminal defense attorneys have been hobbled in their efforts to represent their clients fully and adequately by their own inhibitions. Taking much too seriously their system-inspired designations as "officers of the court," they have succumbed to all of the restrictions that that title necessarily implies, and often forgotten or overlooked the fact that their only legitimate function is as "officers of the client." As a result, they have sat by while their clients are publicly humiliated by court or prosecutor, or consented to procedures or practises that weaken or nullify their defense.

For example, they have permitted so-called gag rules to stand unchallenged and thus cripple any possibility of at least offsetting the prosecution's initial burst of pretrial publicity when the charges are announced to the media. They have acceded to judicial scolding of their clients, often in front of the jury, for such minor peccadilloes as coming late to court or facial or vocal reactions to perjured testimony. They have not taken advantage of opportunities to bring to the attention of the jury facts and circumstances that might significantly affect the verdict.

In many ways, the problems to which I make reference are psychological ones. The law schools and legal commentators, to say nothing of judges and political figures, spend considerable time buttressing the mythology that the law is fair and equitable and that, while there may be sporadic instances of injustice in particular cases, the institution is grounded upon the bedrock of across-the-board due process. Thus, most attorneys come to the bar with a deep-seated belief that they are part and parcel of an ancient and honorable profession and governed by a system of ethical principles that are as all-encompassing as they are lofty.

The reality of the matter is that they are dealing, certainly insofar as the administration of the criminal law is concerned, with what Charles Reich in his best-seller of a few years back, *The Greening of America,* refers to as an inhumane control mechanism designed primarily to protect the interests of what he calls the Corporate State. In every conceivable way, the ending or curtailing of *voir dire* of prospective jurors; the granting to the prosecution of a right to change venue over the defendant's objections; the legalization of less than unanimous verdicts; the imposition of gag rules; the speedy trial regulations; the frequent resort to conspiracy charges; and the curtailment or outright elimination of juries, to name but a handful, the overall system has ensured that criminal defendants get the short end of the stick. In my opinion, the main targets of this process are the Third World minorities who form the cheap labor reservoir that American capitalism is convinced is indispensable to its continuing growth and expansion.

Putting aside the question of the validity of my political conclusions, what can criminal defense attorneys do about the growing number of factors that tend to throttle their natural desire to do the best they can for their clients? Obviously, it is difficult, in any brief paper, to detail the optimum reaction to any set of circumstances that may occur in the courtroom. But one overriding concept can be articulated — the lawyer must start out with the unshakable premise that the odds are neatly stacked against the client, and that the professional prosecutor will do everything that he or she can get away with to lengthen those odds.

With that philosophy in mind, there are certain practical things that can be done. In the first place, both court and prosecution must be convinced that the client is the lawyer's first and only interest. This means that the camaraderie of "The Club" must be avoided. There is nothing that can lessen the ardor of an attorney to fight to the bitter end for a defendant than a relationship with the adversary or the bench that makes real struggle virtually impossible. If this proposition is accepted, it must then follow that the life of a criminal defense attorney is necessarily a relatively lonely one, but the benefits to the client are immense.

Secondly, the lawyers must permit no one — judge, witness or prosecutor — to castigate, embarrass or vilify their clients without a public response, even if the latter are at fault. This pertains to cross-examination and summation as well as judicial spankings. The client and the public must feel that the attorney is so devoted to the former's interests that he or she will risk personal punishment to advance them. If the Chicago conspiracy trial proved nothing else, it sustained this thesis.

Lastly, every possible legal attack on unfair rulings and orders must be mounted before they become final. In this effort, the press must be enlisted as an ally of the defense so that the general public understands what is going on in its courtrooms. The veil of secrecy that cloaks so much prosecutorial and judicial misconduct must be ripped apart by all means necessary if the affected clients are to have even a fighting chance at preserving their liberty or, possibly, their lives.

In short, the advocate for a person accused of crime must live up to every aspect of that term. This does not mean that every prosecution will permit or merit such deep personal involvement, but all practitioners know, almost instinctively, when they have the case that does. If one accepts the basic premise of this paper, then in the appropriate situation, everything else should fall into place. In conclusion, Sir Denis Brogan's remarks at the Bill of Rights Conference sponsored by Long Island University in December of 1966 are certainly appropriate to the arguments advanced above:

> Even if the Bill of Rights does no more than give judges, policemen and even professors a bad conscience from time to time, that is something; if it makes them doubt their infallibility, it is a great deal...

Our efforts may not turn the tide toward universal justice, but they may just possibly give some people bad consciences and enough of such uneasiness can sometimes shake even the highest and seemingly impenetrable of mountains.

CHAPTER FIVE

ON VIOLENCE

THIS LETTER TO THE EDITOR OF THE *NEW YORK TIMES* WAS PUBLISHED ON FEBRUARY 6, 1976. IT WAS WRITTEN IN RESPONSE TO AN EDITORIAL ACCUSING KUNSTLER OF "CONDONING MURDER."

Editor
New York Times
229 West 43rd Street
New York, NY 10036

Dear Sir:

The accusation of "condoning murder" in your recent editorial, because of remarks made by me in Dallas, Texas, is totally false. I do not advocate murder of any sort, and have never condoned those of John and Robert Kennedy. I was as shocked and grieved by their deaths as most Americans. I reject political assassination, except, as I said in Dallas, in the extreme case of an Adolf Hitler.

The essence of my impromptu answers to questions in Dallas was the following: one of the chief causes of violence in our society is the violence of our own government. It has plotted political assassinations of foreign leaders; engaged in foreign invasions; brought death and destruction to hundreds of thousands of innocent people in Southeast Asia; and in that process, taught a generation of Americans to murder. Domestically, governmental violence has been used against disfavored individuals and groups: Attica, Kent State, Chicago and the civil rights struggle.

Almost 50 years ago, Mr. Justice Brandeis warned against governmental misconduct, saying:

> ...Our government is the potent, the omnipresent teacher. For good or for ill, it teaches the whole people by its example. Crime is contagious. If the government becomes a law breaker, it breeds contempt for law; it invites every man to become a law unto himself; it invites anarchy.

Official corruption and violence is equally contagious. America has suffered political assassinations because its leaders have plotted and used those means against others. Recent investigations have revealed that the Kennedys were among the proponents of those tactics.

I have spent most of my professional life developing legal measures as alternatives to more extreme methods of change. I defend political dissidents because I believe a society in which they can survive is a society which can change without violence.

The *New York Times*, which has just successfully upset a court-imposed gag rule, should be the first to acknowledge the value of unfettered freedom – including the freedom to point out the terrible lessons of violence taught us by some of our leaders – however revered they may have been.

Sincerely,
William M. Kunstler

CHAPTER SIX

FBI-TRANSCRIBED SPEECH AT WESTERN KENTUCKY UNIVERSITY

FROM THE FBI FILE: On February 5, 1971, a copy of a tape of a speech made by William Moses Kunstler on February 4, 1971, as maintained in the archives of the Western Kentucky University, was obtained by Special Agent ■ who attended the delivery of this speech on the evening of February 4, 1971, by Kunstler at the Diddle Arena, Western Kentucky University, Bowling Green, Kentucky.

A transcript of the copy of the tape referred to is as follows:

...But I do want to talk about the law not in relationship to Chicago [conspiracy trial] but incorporating Chicago into it. One Supreme Court Justice some years ago, Justice Jackson said that the most oppressive thing in the world is the law being used to oppress, and we have graphic examples now everywhere from the indictment of ■ and others to the Kent State Grand Jury report, to the murder of Fred Hampton in Chicago, to the ■ series of cases, to understand how the law is used. And I say these things I'm going to say not to make you disrespectful of the law (it does that well enough by itself), but to make you understand that the law can be a tyrant and over the eons of history has always been used tyrannically against certain people. Those of you that feel like it, pick up the gospel according to St. Matthew and read of the trial of Christ, a very celebrated political case some 2,000 years ago, for those of you who haven't heard of it.

Christ was tried for the same crime the Chicago defendants were tried for, for dynamiting or threatening to dynamite a building. Though he did not have dynamite – Alfred Nobel hadn't been born yet – the main crime alleged against him was a threat to destroy the temple, stone by stone. And they brought him in before Herod and they tried him, and, as you read Matthew, you find out they ran into a dilemma. All of their informer witnesses contradicted each other and therefore they were in despair what to do about convicting this dangerous revolutionary. So finally they tricked him into testifying against himself, and he obligingly put the words into that record, which Matthew repeats, which convicted him.

Then you will remember that Herod said, "You are convicting an innocent man and I can pardon him, as I have the power to do every Feast of Passover. I can pardon a man convicted of a capital crime."

You will remember that the populace was inflamed by the chief rabbis who said, "Don't pardon him, pardon the other man you have convicted of a capital crime, Barabbas. Give us Barabbas and keep Christ." And the net result was, Barabbas was freed and Christ was executed.

Barabbas's crime was a routine crime: he was guilty of robbery. Christ's crime was a political crime: he was a dangerous revolutionary, who was going up and down the Holy Land telling people such things as "Give away your money, you rich men, and equalize wealth," or, "It is as difficult for a rich man to get into heaven as it is for a camel to pass through the eye of a needle." And he was doing such nonviolent things as throwing money lenders out of the temple, and he was doing exactly what Jerry Rubin advocates. He is telling the people he wanted to separate father from son and mother from daughter, and that he had come not with peace but a sword. He was a danger and rightfully so, and so he was destroyed by informers, by the corruption of his friends.

Judas Iscariot was corrupted by the system to point him out with a kiss to the soldiers, and then in his own despair, to take the 30 pieces of silver and try to buy his friend back from Pharisees, and then hanged himself when he was unsuccessful. He was virtually betrayed by Peter, who three times before the cock crowed, disowned him. All of the aspects of any political trial, but it was the law that condemned Jesus Christ, not an assassin in the dark; a legal process resulting in a legal execution of a man whose crime was words, whose crime was ideas.

Socrates the same. His crime was corrupting the morals of the youth of Athens and he took the hemlock after a court decree that found him guilty. It's the same all the way through history. Every Jew that went to a gas chamber went with a neatly typed extermination decree of a German court. Every Dreyfus who went to a Devil's Island went with some decree of a court or a court martial. Every Sacco and Vanzetti, every Tom Mooney, every Eugene Debs – all the same, with a neatly typed or inscribed court decree. And the terrible danger of all of this is that people tend to want to believe that if it is legal, it is right. Those two words, legality and justice, are miles apart. A legal decree does not mean justice, rightness, righteousness. And I think that if I leave nothing behind me tonight to memorialize this particular evening, I hope I leave you with skepticism about courts and about decrees. I'd like to discuss a few that are more contemporary than a trial 2,000 or so years ago in Jerusalem.

At Kent State last year, between May 1 and May 4, a student

body witnessed four murders on the campus. Two men and two women students were blown apart with M-1 rifles. Nine other students were wounded, four of them permanently, one crippled for life, and the other had half his foot blown away. And there are other medical facts, which we don't have to go into. You remember the effect on the country of Kent State and then its follow-up at Jackson State, with two young black men, not as well publicized as four white students because our values are quite different in that respect, but at least through its juxtaposition with Kent State, fairly well known. Two Grand Juries were impaneled at both places. At Kent State a ROTC building had been burned, the National Guard had been called out. They were on the commons. They went down the hill toward a practise football field, driving student demonstrators before them. Then they went up the hill where they grouped and formed. The students were literally hundreds of yards away. A shot rang out and the National Guard opened fire on the students and I don't have to go into the details. You saw that [young] girl screaming over the body of one of them.

There was called into being, shortly thereafter, a Grand Jury of Portage County, Ohio, and the Grand Jury returned with indictments last fall indicting 25 students and faculty members – 24 students, one faculty member – accusing them of causing the Kent State tragedy, and indicting them for a whole series of crimes: riot, inciting to riot, and so on. That Grand Jury report was just held by a Federal Court to be unconstitutional, to have destroyed the chance of these young people for any sort of a fair trial. But the prosecutor, who had publicly announced after the Grand Jury report was returned that he was sorry the National Guard didn't kill them all, said he is going ahead anyway with the underlying indictments.

But the fact of the matter is that an agency of the government, a Grand Jury that is supposed to be protection from the law to the citizen, was used as a deliberate instrument of oppression. It said only one word or two about the National Guard in its entire report.

It said that the National Guard, while it had been justified in firing, because there had been a student sniper (that later turned out to be a shot from a Beretta pistol in the hands of the major of the National Guard in command of the unit) – the only word of criticism against the National Guard was that an M-1 rifle was too heavy a caliber for student bodies. That's because Sandy Sawyer's coffin had to be shut because her face was blown away by an M-1 shell. And they recommended possibly .22 caliber guns in the future for student demonstrators. So you had murder sanctified by a Grand Jury and yet students are asked to believe and trust the law, that it will protect you, it will be your shield. That's incident #1...

On January 30, [1933], Adolf Hitler was named by a sick and ailing president, Hindenburg, to be chancellor of Germany, but he did not have a majority in the Reichstag, although he had the largest number of votes in the Reichstag, 37 percent. There were elections in March of 1933, the last elections in Germany for virtually a decade and a half. At those elections the Nazi Party lost ground. It had gone up in February to 42 percent and down in March to 41 percent, and Hitler did not have a mandate to begin a nightmare, a world nightmare, and so a political trial was necessary.

And so a half-mad Dutch youth by the name of Vanderlover was escorted to a tunnel from Hermann Goering's house to the Reichstag, the symbol of German unity, with two cans of kerosene, and he started a fire that burned that building down. And the next thing you knew, there was a trial of Vanderlover, yes, this half-witted young man from Holland, but with him the leaders of the Communist Party in Germany, who had, next to the Nazi Party, the largest bloc in the Reichstag. And chief among them was a man named Georgi Dimitrov, a Bulgarian who had come to Germany and reconstituted the German Communist Party. Dimitrov was tried and courts were still open then, still free, because Hitler did not have his mandate and could not replace the original

German judges that were there when he became chancellor.

Dimitrov was tried. He utilized the subpoena power that defendants had, and he subpoenaed Herman Goering to the stand. Dimitrov acted as his own lawyer. He destroyed Goering on the stand. He forced Goering to admit that Goering had burnt the Reichstag. And Goering walked off the stand before they had finished questioning him, and said to Dimitrov, "I'll get you in the streets." But the German court acquitted Dimitrov, condemned Vanderlover, who was then beheaded in the restoration of the public guillotining – one of the great reforms that Hitler instituted after the burning of the Reichstag.

But even though Dimitrov was acquitted, Vanderlover's execution, coupled with a mounting diatribe against the Communist Party, linking it in the public mind with the burning of the Reichstag, led Germans to believe that if the communists could burn and destroy – this party that had some 35 percent of the German vote – anyone could do it, and we need now law and order in Germany.

And that was the beginning of a nightmare that was eventually to cost 22 million lives, and destroy civilization and destroy a little bit of every one of us for a long time to come. It came through a judicial process. It was the utilization of something the Germans said was legal. It wasn't taking Dimitrov off and assassinating him – that came later. It wasn't beating people in the streets without rhyme or reason – that came later. It was convincing people through a judicial process that Christ was reborn and dangerous again. It was utilizing the courts, the mechanism, the legality to make any crime tolerable. Out of it came an epoch which is indescribable but which can come again.

Human history is not unique from episode to episode. You may not believe Toynbee's cyclical theory of history, but it is recurrent and the judicial process is very much tied up with some of its most awesome recurrences. Repeatedly, those in power in our country have been successful in convincing Middle America that there is an utter danger in certain people. George Orwell had a character known as Goldstein in *1984,* whom Big Brother kept alive as an enemy of the state to remind the people whom he watched through these television receivers that he was protecting them against the awful enemy, this fabricated enemy, Goldstein, who was deliberately kept alive to be a symbol of every man and woman's most pressing fears. And because they were afraid of this Goldstein, the people tolerated the noose being placed gently around their necks until it was too late to move. That is exactly what happens and is happening now...

The German people were not ogres and monsters. The German people were no different than you are. You have no claim – and when I say you I mean all of us – have no claim that we are better or more righteous people than any other people on Earth. That we have better instincts, that we're finer human beings, we're all the same. When the fright's grown and you permit it to grow, you too will tolerate any indecency, if you are afraid enough.

And the terrible part of it all is that all of the violence, all of the inhumanity is practised by those who point the finger at you, the Panthers and the Weatherpeople and say they are violent. Ask yourselves some very interesting questions. Ask yourself whether you believe the Black Panthers started the war in Southeast Asia, or pilot the B-52 planes. Was it the American students or the Weatherpeople that went to My Lai? Was it the students and the Black Panthers that put hard hats on and bludgeoned 87 people into the hospital for doing nothing but walking up and down the steps of the Sub-Treasury Building with signs against the war in Vietnam last fall? Did the Panthers shoot the four at Kent State or the two at Jackson State? Did the students murder Fred Hampton? Do they fly the B-52s every day or defoliate the Vietnamese countryside? Are the Black Panthers marching up the Laotian border tonight and extending the war one step further, this mad and indescribable war?

Where are the real bloodstained hands? Isn't it much more

likely that they are thumping the Oval [Office] table than that they are in black homes in the ghetto or on campuses? Where are the real murderers and the real violent oppressors? Who is doing the destroying, and the murdering and the wounding? Who is causing such rents in our society and in the fabric of what we live by?

I think you ought to ask yourself those questions when your president says students are violent – when the pot calls the kettle black. I say these things not to be overly dramatic, because I think to be overly dramatic is maybe to add to the general hysteria. I say them because I feel them and I sense they are true. I am not a seer or a prophet and I have no more brains or insight or foresight than any other man or woman. I ask you to consider them, what has been said, not to be stampeded by me or anyone else, and to reach reasoned conclusions of your own. There is a tendency to treat you as some sort of sheep, that any speaker can come and fill your head with ideas and that you will then react in a primordial way. I have far too much respect for you to think that I or anyone else can or should do that. You have to analyze for yourselves, you cannot afford any longer to let anyone else do that for you – not your parents, your teachers or any other group or person. You have to decide. You have to reach certain conclusions.

I think that this issue of violence on your part or the part of the other groups or individuals I mentioned is being used politically and ethically to destroy; to bring about a situation in which all governmental policies, all of the system's excesses, will pass without opposition, first subtly, and then not so subtly. And there is a chance that at some time, somewhere in the future, we will suddenly wake up one sad and tragic morning and hear those same boots at the door that the Germans began to hear after 1934, and say to ourselves, "My God, did it happen? Where did we go wrong? Why can't we fight back?" But then it's much too late, and then it's all gone and you and I may have to live out another nightmare until it comes right again. That should not happen to human beings.

We have now the ability to fight, it is not Germany in 1934, we're before that time, but so were the Germans once. Do you think any German, if you had taken a poll in any city – Munich, Bonn, Berlin, Leipzig – in 1933, 1932, and stopped people on the street with your little yellow pad and said, "Miss, do you believe that within a year and one half there will be such things as concentration camps, a Dachau, and Bergen-Belsen, Auschwitz, Treblinka? Do you believe that lampshades, in your name, will be made of human skin? Do you believe that human beings will be stripped of their clothing and immersed for hours in freezing water, so that the German army's uniforms for next winter's campaign will be more scientifically fabricated? Do you believe that gold fillings will be chipped out of the dead mouths of human beings so that your country can go to war with three-quarters of the world? Do you believe that Jews by the millions, and other East Europeans and others will be marched in your name into shower rooms only to be destroyed by Zyklon B gas? Can you believe that 22 million people will die in your name?" – and I am sure nobody would say, "Yes, I can believe those things."

You have to ask yourselves without becoming overly frightened or overly hysterical – if it can happen there, it can happen here. If one nation can go mad, so can another. But it doesn't come overnight. It is not a sudden climactic epidemic sickness. It is the accumulation of the loss of bits of freedom everywhere that suddenly bring that strange and tragic morning I referred to.

You must band together as the Germans never did. You must find a common unity as young people who have more to fear in a way because you've got a longer road to run. You must find a unity that is different than the German unity. They found theirs in bulldozed mass raids throughout Europe. That kind of unity doesn't help anybody but maggots and earthworms. You've got to find it here, not in ideological unity, not a tactical unity, but you must spring to the defense of every group or organization or individual that you honestly feel is being persecuted by this system through its judicial process, because if you desert one, you will be in the same position that Pastor Niemöller so poignantly illustrated when he said, "When they came for the Jews, I did not cry out because I was not a Jew." You can't afford, for the sake of your lives and everything you want out of the sweetness and decency of this world, to let that occur.

CHAPTER SEVEN

FBI-TRANSCRIBED SPEECH IN BOWLING GREEN, KENTUCKY

KUNSTLER SPOKE TO STUDENTS IN BOWLING GREEN, KENTUCKY ON APRIL 2, 1971. THE FBI TAPED AND TRANSCRIBED THE FOLLOWING EXCERPT, WHICH BILL LIKED TO RECALL AS A HIGHLIGHT OF THE TRIAL OF THE CHICAGO SEVEN CASE.

FROM THE FBI FILE: There was one episode, which I thought probably symbolized a lot about life-styles. A package came to the defense table one day, about the fifth or sixth week in the trial. We thought it was a package of hair, because at the beginning of the trial one of the Yippie pamphlets that went out, one of the fliers, was for hair for Jerry and Julius. Jerry had had his hair shaved while serving a term in Santa Rita in California for an old sit-in conviction, and Julius, the judge, had by the attrition of many centuries lost most of his. So for two weeks hair came to our table in every conceivable shape and form. And from every conceivable part of the human body. In fact, one of the little games we played before the judge came in, was to pick up a package here and there of the pounds that came and try to decipher from where it came.

You know, sex, race, etc.

Well, a package came a couple of weeks after the hair died down. It was delivered by the judge's bailiff. It was addressed to Abbie and Jerry, care of Julius, Federal Building, Chicago, Illinois. And Abbie opened it, and out of it spilled on the table not hair at all but a greenish tobacco-like substance. Some of the cognoscenti at the table smelled it, and I heard all sorts of things like, "It's Tanganyika black," "It's Jamaica red," and so on. I smelled it, and it was more like Accapucolo [*sic*] gold *(applause)*. My apologies to David Fry.

But in any event, we put a copy of the *Berkeley Barb* over it because it was three and a half ounces of what looked like quite good grass. And we had 30 marshals in the room, FBI agents, the judge, Chicago policemen. And the question was: with the life-style of most of the defendants, what do you [do] about that grass at the end of the day? Do you slink away and leave it for the marshals? Do you just package it and walk out? Or do you try to legalize the situation? So the theory at the table was, since the government was legalizing persecution, we would legalize grass.

And so I made a motion, the last motion of the day. The marshal was ready to gavel us out of existence for that day. And I said, "Your Honor, there has been delivered to us some grass."

He looked blank.

I said, "Your Honor, some cannabis. Which is what the statute calls it."

"Aha," he said. ■■■■

I said, "Your Honor, it was delivered to us by your bailiff." *(applause)* And I said, "I would like instructions as to its disposition."

He said, "Mr. Kunstler, you're a very resolute attorney and I am sure that you will know how to dispose of it."

I said, "Your Honor, as an officer of the court, I give you my solemn word that it will be burnt tonight." *(considerable glee)*

By that time the marshal, Dubowski, had put his gavel down,

court was adjourned, Weinglass and I are standing up at the lectern. We turn around with a certain amount of anticipation. There wasn't a client left at the table, and not one shred of the cannabis was in existence. But in the morning I assured the judge – because I received some reasonable proof that it had been burnt – I assured the judge that it had been properly disposed of. And that signified the end of the incident.

CHAPTER EIGHT

SUMMATION FOR THE DEFENSE IN THE CHICAGO SEVEN TRIAL

THE CHICAGO EIGHT*

Director Hoover thought the time was due
To put the New Left on the thorny path,
So he invoked the aid of Nixon's crew
In directing the Presidential wrath.

From SDS he picked a likely pair,
And then two Yippie chieftains swelled the list
Filled by a teacher and the Panther chair,
A student and an aging pacifist.

The trial went on for almost a half a year,
While witness after witness took the stand
To try to justify J. Edgar's fear
That those accused were perils to the land.

But, at the end, the jury found them free
Of any traces of conspiracy.

---

*KUNSTLER WROTE THIS ABOUT THE CHICAGO EIGHT IN A COLLECTION OF SONNETS ENTITLED *TRIALS AND TRIBULATIONS*, GROVE PRESS (NEW YORK, 1985).

CLOSING ARGUMENT FOR THE DEFENDANTS BY MR. KUNSTLER, FEBRUARY 12 AND 13, 1970.

MR. KUNSTLER: Ladies and Gentlemen of the jury.

This is the last voice that you will hear from the defense. We have no rebuttal. This government has the last word. In an introductory fashion I would just like to state that only you will judge this case as far as the facts go. This is your solemn responsibility and it is an awesome one.

After you have heard Mr. Schultz and Mr. Weinglass, there must be lots of questions running in your minds. You have seen the same scenes described by two different people. You have heard different interpretations of those scenes by two different people. But you are the ones that draw the final inference. You will be the ultimate arbiters of the fate of these seven men.

In deciding this case we are relying upon your oath of office and that you will decide it only on the facts, not on whether you like the lawyers or don't like the lawyers. We are really quite unimportant. Whether you like the judge or don't like the judge, that is unimportant, too. Whether you like the defendants or don't like the defendants.

THE COURT: I am glad you didn't say I was unimportant.

MR. KUNSTLER: No. The likes or dislikes are unimportant.

And I can say that it is not whether you like the defendants or don't like the defendants. You may detest all of the defendants, for all I know; you may love all of them, I don't know. It is unimportant. It shouldn't interfere with your decision, it shouldn't come into it. And this is hard to do.

You have seen a long defense here. There have been harsh things said in this court, and harsh things to look at from your jury box. You have seen a man bound and gagged. You have heard lots of things that are probably all not pleasant. Some of them have been humorous. Some have been bitter. Some may have been downright boring, and I imagine many were. Those things really shouldn't influence your decision. You have an oath to decide the facts and to decide them divorced of any personal considerations of your own, and I remind you that if you don't do that, you will be living a lie the rest of your life, and only you will be living with that lie.

Now, I don't think it has been any secret to you that the defendants have some questions as to whether they are receiving a fair trial. That has been raised many times.

MR. FORAN: Your Honor, I object to this.

THE COURT: I sustain the objection.

MR. KUNSTLER: They stand here indicted under a new statute. In fact, the conspiracy, which is Count I, starts the day after the president signed the law.

MR. FORAN: Your Honor, I object to that. The law is for the Court to determine, not for counsel to determine.

THE COURT: I sustain the objection.

MR. KUNSTLER: Your Honor, I am not going into the law. They have a right to know when it was passed.

THE COURT: I don't want my responsibility usurped by you.

MR. KUNSTLER: I want you to know, first that these defendants had a constitutional right to travel. They have a constitutional right to dissent and to agitate for dissent. No one would deny that, not Mr. Foran, and not I, or anyone else.

Just some 50 years ago, I think almost exactly, in a criminal court building here in Chicago, Clarence Darrow said this:

> When a truth comes upon the earth, or a great idea necessary for mankind is born, where does it come from? Not from the police force, or the prosecuting attorneys, or the judges, or the lawyers, or the doctors. Not there. It comes from the despised and the outcasts, and it comes perhaps from jails and prisons. It comes from men who have dared to be rebels and think their thoughts, and their faith has been the faith of rebels.
>
> What do you suppose would have happened to the working men except for these rebels all the way down through history? Think of the complacent cowardly people who never raise their voices against the powers that be. If there had been only these, you gentlemen of the jury would be hewers of wood and drawers of water. You gentlemen would have been slaves. You gentlemen owe whatever you have and whatever you hope to these brave rebels who dared to think, and dared to speak, and dared to act.

This was Clarence Darrow 50 years ago in another case.

You don't have to look for rebels in other countries. You can just look at the history of this country.

You will recall that there was a great demonstration that took place around the Customs House in Boston in 1770. It was a demonstration of the people of Boston against the people who were enforcing the Sugar Act, the Stamp Act, the Quartering of Troops Act. And they picketed at one place where it was important to be, at the Customs House where the customs were collected.

You remember the testimony in this case. Superintendent Rochford said, "Go up to Lincoln Park, go to the band shell, go anywhere you want, but don't go to the amphitheatre."

That was like telling the Boston patriots, "Go anywhere you

want, but don't go to the Customs House." Because it was at the Customs House and it was at the amphitheatre that the protesters wanted to show that something was terribly and totally wrong. They wanted to show it at the place it was important, and so the seeming compliance of the city in saying, "Go anywhere you want throughout the city. Go to Jackson Park. Go to Lincoln Park," has no meaning. That is an excuse for preventing a demonstration at the single place that had meaning, which was the amphitheatre.

The Customs House in Boston was the scene of evil and so the patriots demonstrated. They ran into a Chicago. You know what happened. The British soldiers shot them down and killed five of them, including one black man, Crispus Atticus, who was the first man to die, by the way, in the American Revolution. They were shot down in the street by the British for demonstrating at the Customs House.

You will remember that after the Boston Massacre, which was the name the Colonists gave to it, all sorts of things happened in the Colonies. There were all sorts of demonstrations…

MR. FORAN: Your Honor, I have sat here quite a while and I object to this. This is not a history lecture. The purpose of summation is to sum up the facts of the case and I object to this.

THE COURT: I do sustain the objection. Unless you get down to evidence, I will direct you to discontinue this lecture on history. We are not dealing with history.

MR. KUNSTLER: But to understand the overriding issues as well, Your Honor...

THE COURT: I will not permit any more of these historical references and I direct you to discontinue them, sir.

MR. KUNSTLER: I do so under protest, Your Honor. I will get down, because the judge has prevented me from going into material that I wanted to…

MR. FORAN: Your Honor, I object to that comment.

THE COURT: I have not prevented you. I have ruled properly as a matter of law. The law prevents you from doing it, sir.

MR. KUNSTLER: I will get down to the evidence in this case. I am going to confine my remarks to showing you how the government stoops to conquer in this case.

The prosecution recognized early that if you were to see 33 police officers in uniform take the stand [then] you would realize how much of the case depends on law enforcement officers. So they strip the uniforms from those witnesses, and you notice you began to see almost an absence of uniforms. Even the Deputy Police Chief came without a uniform.

Mr. Schultz said, "Look at our witnesses. They don't argue with the judge. They are bright and alert. They sit there and they answer clearly."

They answered like automatons – one after the other, robots took the stand.

"Did you see any missiles?"

"A barrage." (Everybody saw a barrage of missiles.)

"What were the demonstrators doing?"

"Screaming. Indescribably loud."

"What were they screaming?"

"Profanities of all sorts."

I call your attention to James Murray. That is the reporter, and this is the one they got caught with. This is the one that slipped up. James Murray, who is a friend of the police, who thinks the police are the steadying force in Chicago. This man came to the stand, and he wanted you to rise up when you heard "Viet Cong flags," this undeclared war we are fighting against an undeclared enemy. He wanted you to think that the march from Grant Park into the center of Chicago in front of the Conrad Hilton was a march run by the Viet Cong, or have the Viet Cong flags so infuriate you that you would feel against these demonstrators that they were less than human beings. The only problem is that he never saw any Viet Cong flags. First of all, there were none, and I call your attention to the movies, and if you see one Viet Cong flag in those two hours of movies at Michigan and Balbo, you can call me a liar and convict my clients.

Mr. Murray, under whatever instructions were given to him, or under his own desire to help the Police Department, saw them. I asked him a simple question: describe them. Remember what he said? "They are black."

Then he heard laughter in the courtroom because there isn't a person in the room that thinks the Viet Cong flag is a black flag. He heard a twitter in the courtroom. He said, "No, they are red."

Then he heard a little more laughter.

Then I said, "Are they all red?"

He said, "No, they have some sort of a symbol on them."

"What is the symbol?"

"I can't remember."

When you look at the pictures, you won't even see any black flags at Michigan and Balbo. You will see some red flags, two of them, I believe, and I might say to you that a red flag was the flag under which General Washington fought at the Battle of Brandywine, a flag made for him by the nuns of Bethlehem.

I think after what Murray said you can disregard his testimony. He was a clear liar on the stand. He did a lot of things they wanted him to do. He wanted people to say things that you could hear that would make you think these demonstrators were violent people. He had some really rough ones in there. He had, "The Hump Sucks," "Daley Sucks the Hump" — pretty rough expressions. He didn't have "Peace Now." He didn't hear that. He didn't give you any others. Oh, I think he had "Charge. The street is ours. Let's go."

That is what he wanted you to hear. He was as accurate about that as he was about the Viet Cong flag, and remember his testimony about the whiffle balls. One injured his leg. Others he picked up. Where were those whiffle balls in this courtroom? You know what a whiffle ball is. It is something you can hardly throw. Why didn't the government let you see the whiffle ball? They didn't let you see it because it can't be thrown. They didn't let you see it because the nails are shiny. I got a glimpse of it. Why didn't you see it? They want you to see a photograph so you can see that the nails don't drop out on the photograph. We never saw any of these weapons. That is enough for Mr. Murray. I have, I think, wasted more time than he is worth on Mr. Murray.

Now I have one witness to discuss with you who is extremely important and gets us into the alleged attack on the Grant Park underground garage.

This is the most serious plan that you have had. This is more serious than attacking the pigs, as they tried to pin onto the Yippies and the National Mobe. This is to bomb. This is frightening, this concept of bombing an underground garage, probably the most frightening concept that you can imagine.

By the way, Grant Park garage is impossible to bomb with Molotov cocktails. It is a pure concrete garage. You won't find a stick of wood in it, if you go there. But, put that aside for the moment. In a mythical tale, it doesn't matter that buildings won't burn.

In judging the nonexistence of this so-called plot, you must remember the following things.

Lieutenant Healy in his vigil, supposedly, in the garage, never saw anything in anybody's hands, not in Shimabukuro's, whom he says he saw come into the garage, not in Lee Weiner's hands, whom he said he saw come into the garage, or any of the other four or five people whom he said he saw come into the garage. These people that he said he saw come into the garage were looking, he said, in two cars. What were they looking into cars for? You can ask that question. Does that testimony make any sense, that they come in empty-handed into a garage, these people who you are supposed to believe were going to fire bomb the underground garage?

Just keep that in mind when you consider this fairy tale when you are in the jury room.

Secondly, in considering it you have the testimony of Lieutenant Healy, who never saw Lee Wiener before. You remember he said, "I never saw him before. I had looked at some pictures they had shown me."

But he never had seen him and he stands in a stairwell behind a closed door looking through a one-foot-by-one-foot opening in that door, with chicken wire across it and a double layer of glass, for three to four seconds, he said, and he could identify what he said was Lee Wiener in three to four seconds across what he said was 30 to 40 yards away.

MR. FORAN: Your Honor, I object to "three or four seconds." It was five minutes.

MR. KUNSTLER: No, sir. The testimony reads, Your Honor, that he identified him after three or four seconds and if Mr. Foran will look...

MR. FORAN: Then he looked at him for five minutes.

MR. KUNSTLER: He identified him after three or four seconds.

THE COURT: Do you have the transcript there?

MR. FORAN: Your Honor, I would accept that. He identified him immediately but he was looking at him for five minutes.

MR. KUNSTLER: I just think you ought to consider that in judging Lieutenant Healy's question. This officer was not called before the Grand Jury investigating that very thing. And I think you can judge the importance of that man's testimony on whether he ever did tell the United States Attorney anything about this in September of 1968.

I submit he didn't because it didn't happen. It never happened. This is a simple fabrication. The simple truth of the matter is that there never was any such plot and you can prove it to yourselves. Nothing was ever found, there is not visible proof of this at all. No bottles. No rags. No sand. No gasoline. It was supposed to be a diversionary tactic, Mr. Schultz told you in his summation. This was a diversionary tactic. Diversionary to what? This was Thursday night.

If you will recall, the two marches to the Amphitheatre that got as far as 16th and 18th Streets on Michigan had occurred earlier. The only thing that was left was the Downers Grove picnic. It was a diversionary operation to divert attention from the picnic at Downers Grove. It was diversionary to nothing. The incident lives only in conversations, the two conversations supposedly overheard by Frapolly and Bock, who are the undercover agents who were characterized, I thought, so aptly by Mr. Weinglass.

Now just a few more remarks. One, I want to tell you that as jurors, as I have already told you, you have a difficult task. But you also have the obligation, if you believe that these seven men are not guilty, to stand on that, and it doesn't matter that other jurors feel the other way. If you honestly and truly believe it, you must stand and you must not compromise on that stand.

MR. FORAN: Your Honor, I object to that. Your Honor will instruct the jury what their obligations are.

THE COURT: I sustain the objection. You are getting into my part of the job.

MR. KUNSTLER: What you do in that jury room, no one can question you on. It is up to you. You don't have to answer as to it to anybody and you must stand firm if you believe either way and not...

MR. FORAN: Your Honor, I object to that.

THE COURT: I sustain the objection. I told you not to talk about that, Mr. Kunstler.

MR. KUNSTLER: I think I have a right to do it.

THE COURT: You haven't a right when the Court tells you not to, and it is a matter of law that is peculiarly my function. You may not tell the jury what the law is.

MR. KUNSTLER: Before I come to my final conclusion, I want to thank you both for myself, for Mr. Weinglass and for our clients, for your attention. It has been an ordeal for you, I know. We are sorry that it had to be so. But we are grateful that you have listened. We know you will weigh, free of any prejudice on any level, because if you didn't, then the jury system would be destroyed and would have no meaning whatsoever. We are living in extremely troubled times, as Mr. Weinglass pointed out. An intolerable war abroad has divided and dismayed us all. Racism at home and poverty at home are both causes of despair and discouragement. In a so-called affluent society, we have people starving, and people who can't even begin to approximate the decent life.

These are rough problems, terrible problems, and as has been said by everybody in this country, they are so enormous that they stagger the imagination. But they don't go away by destroying their critics. They don't vanish by sending men to jail. They never did and they never will.

To use these problems by attempting to destroy those who protest against them is probably the most indecent thing that we can do. You can crucify a Jesus, you can poison a Socrates, you can hang John Brown or Nathan Hale, you can kill a Che Guevara, you can jail a Eugene Debs or a Bobby Seale. You can assassinate John Kennedy or a Martin Luther King, but the problems remain. The solutions are essentially made by continuing and perpetuating with every breath; you have the right of men to think, the right of men to speak boldly and unafraid, the right to be masters of their souls, the right to live free and to die free. The hangman's rope never solved a single problem except that of one man.

I think if this case does nothing else, perhaps it will bring into focus that again we are in that moment of history when a courtroom becomes the proving ground of whether we do live free and whether we do die free. You are in that position now. Suddenly all importance has shifted to you – shifted to you as I guess in the last analysis it should go, and it is really your responsibility, I think, to see that men remain able to think, to speak boldly and unafraid, to be masters of their souls, and to live and die free. And perhaps if you do what is right, perhaps Allen Ginsberg will never have to write again as he did in *Howl,* "I saw the best minds of my generation destroyed by madness." Perhaps Judy Collins will never have to stand in any courtroom again and say as she did, "When will they ever learn? When will they ever learn?"

CHAPTER NINE

FBI-TRANSCRIBED SPEECH IN JACKSONVILLE, FLORIDA

THE FBI RECORDED AND TRANSCRIBED THIS SPEECH ON NOVEMBER 5, 1970. IT WAS DELIVERED AT THE CIVIC AUDITORIUM IN JACKSONVILLE, FLORIDA. WE REPRINT PERTINENT EXCERPTS CONCERNING VIOLENCE BELOW.

FROM THE FBI FILE: ■ Civic Auditorium, Jacksonville, Florida, recorded the speech delivered by William Kunstler at the Civic Auditorium on the evening of November 5, 1970, and furnished this tape recording to an agent of the Federal Bureau of Investigation. A transcript of that speech taken from the above tape as well as a tape recording made by a Special Agent of the Federal Bureau of Investigation follows:

... The governing body in this country today is creating a mythical violence and they are using the actual threat of violence to create some of the most dangerous illusions that any society has ever created. They are saying, in effect, and the last election was just one good example of it, they are saying, in effect, that there is running amuck in this country, in their burning ghettos and in their embittered campuses, a new breed of evil-doer. There is running amuck a most dangerous animal, the militant black, the radical white and the demonstrating student; and that these animals must be crushed by whatever means are necessary. And I will give you some examples of how this is operating and how dangerous it is.

You have all read, I am sure, *1984* in which Orwell many years ago in Big Brother's land created a public enemy. I think his name was Goldstein, and the object of Goldstein in the Orwellian sense was to have a public enemy who would be visible in an invisible way to the general community. "There is your enemy. We are protecting you against him. Unless you support us, he will overwhelm you; therefore, support us and we will keep Goldstein in check."

For what's happened has been a deliberate campaign to create a country of Goldsteins. We call them students. We call them Panthers. We call them white radicals, members of SDS, Weathermen, whatever it happens to be. And that group is utilized to disguise where the real violence exists, and not the violence of self-defense, which is on a relatively minor scale, but the real violence, the real blood-letting that exists, of course, in Vietnam, and in the ghettos, and on the campuses, that exists in Song Mei, at Kent State, at Jackson State, and Augusta, Georgia, all of which have been mentioned tonight; that exists on the steps of the Sub-Treasury Building in New York, that exists when bullets explode in the brains of Kennedys and Martin Luther King and Medgar Evers, Viola Liuzzo and Jim Reeves, on Highway 80 between Selma and Montgomery; that exists in what happens throughout the poverty-stricken areas of this country; that exists throughout, in churches in Birmingham and in other areas of the country. And to disguise that and to perpetuate that, the mythical violence is created. The outlaw is created, an outlaw band, an outlaw band of Goldsteins and in that group you have many people, many of whom are familiar to you.

You have a Fred Hampton, he is in that group; and because of Fred Hampton, [he] becomes a symbol of the mythical violence that they see at the hands of the black community. He is murdered in his bed by a posse of detectives ostensibly on a hunt for weapons, a routine hunt for weapons. One of the detectives even testified, "I didn't even know that it was a Black Panther house that we were breaking into." And so they entered the house on West Monroe Street in Chicago and they murdered two men, two very young men. A man named Mark Clark, who was in his teens, and a man named Fred Hampton. Hampton was asleep in his bed and he becomes a victim of this Goldstein psychology. The dominant community in Chicago breathes easier because a Goldstein had been put away. No one, of course, is indicted, even though a Federal Grand Jury finds that murder was done. Nobody is indicted for the simple reason, says the Grand Jury, that no Panthers [unintelligible].

It is, one, to remind the dominant community that Big Brother will take care of the misfits, and then secondly, it is to remind those who are questioning the dominant community's values that they might be lying on the commons of Kent State themselves if they persist. They might be lying face down in the streets of Augusta if they persist. They might be lying in Alexander Hall in a pool of blood if they persist. This is an effective technique. It's important to understand it and to see why it's operating. The Nazis used the Reichstag. That was a method of creating Goldsteins. We use shoot-outs. We use television sets. We use demonstrations on the college campus to get much the same reaction...

Well, the question is, what do we do about all of this? Well, some people are taking very strong measures. Some people are resorting to dynamite and Molotov cocktails. There is a group, the

Weathermen to name one, who have become so embittered and frustrated that they are now utilizing terroristic methods. Well, terrorism has a place. It always has had. I am not sure that now is the time for it, because my reading of history always indicated that it was best used when there was a chance for a transfer of power: such as the Israelis used in Palestine in 1945 and 1946, doing such "nonviolent" things as blowing up the King David Hotel, among others. The Algerians used it in the streets of Algiers in 1954 and 1955. The American colonists used it from 1766 to 1776 and beyond, and other countries and other societies have used it, but always at a time [when] it was to be successful, when there was a reasonable chance for a change in power.

I don't think we are at that stage right now, but on the other hand, I would not in any way put the Weathermen down or desert them or in any way hold myself aloof from their needs. I think their goals are much the same as my own. I may differ with methods, but at this point, only as to time of use. I would hope that perhaps the methods they think now are useful would never come to pass. But I am no longer prepared to say that they will not come to pass. I think everything done by the dominant culture almost makes them inevitable, because what is being done speaks to bitterness and frustration and tells people that there is no use [in waiting].

CHAPTER TEN

FBI-TRANSCRIBED SPEECH IN SAN JOSE, CALIFORNIA

FROM THE FBI FILE: First source advised on May 26, 1970, that Associated Student Body, San José State College, San José, California, had invited William Kunstler to speak at San José State College on the evening of May 26, 1970. ████ the California State College System, █████ issued an order canceling the Kunstler appearance due to the possibility of violence.

On May 26, 1970, U.S. District Judge Robert Peckham, San Francisco, California, issued an order prohibiting San José State College ███ from canceling the Kunstler speech. Kunstler appeared at San José State College at 7:30 p.m., on May 26, 1970.

A second source advised on May 26, 1970, that William Kunstler spoke at 7 – 7th Street on the San José State College Campus on May 26, 1970. He spoke from 8:00 p.m. to 8:40 p.m. There were approximately 3,000 persons in attendance, mostly white and of student age.

There was no violence, arrests or property damage during this activity. After Kunstler's speech, the crowd dispersed quietly. There were no uniformed police in evidence.

The following is a transcript of Kunstler's speech provided by the second source above.

...When I stand here and I say to you that a young man who cooperates with the draft is cooperating with the immorality and indecency of a war which in turn is a microcosm of all the evils of our own society, I am breaking a law. I am breaking the law that Dr. [Benjamin] Spock was assumed to have broken. I guess I'm counseling that you should avoid the draft and that is a federal crime, but I don't think that I can stand here and protect myself by utilizing weasel-like words to avoid saying what I believe and think. And if the price of that is the federal prison, that has to be the price. But you've got to start thinking in terms of price yourself, because it's not enough to sit and applaud me or anyone else. Those things mean very little. They make you feel warm inside and I must confess they make me feel warm inside, but this is not a time to try to mutually comfort each other.

Now is the time for action, for movement, and the movement is where you are, the power is where you are and you've got to exercise it. Now that doesn't mean breaking a few windows downtown or anywhere else. Those things accomplish nothing. They're worse than nothing. They bring the nightsticks out and they bring out the provocateurs who want nothing more than a clash between young people and the police. You've lived through that, Berkeley has lived through that, Columbia has lived through that, Kent State, Jackson State, Orangeburg, all throughout the United States. So many of our people are either underground, like the Weathermen, or are suffering the memories of a split head, whether it be in Chicago, San José or anywhere else. Those things only give [weight to] the lunatic fringe in this country, which tries to inflate what students do with violence: even though in all of its cumulative moments, it amounts to a few broken windows in a few buildings around the country.

They try to say our students are violent. Well, students didn't kill Martin Luther King, or President Kennedy, or Robert Kennedy, or the four at Kent State or the two at Jackson State or the seven in Augusta or Martin Luther King or Malcolm X or Medgar Evers. Who the hell is committing the real violence in America? It's never the students or the left wing. Then try to calculate how many windows are broken every time a B-52 flies over South Vietnam and you'll get some understanding of real violence.

But don't let them provoke you into the paddy wagons or into the hospital, because that is exactly what is desired. That's the reason behind most of the true violence that occurs. That's the reason behind the provocateurs who want to push you into the path of a bullet or a billyclub because they know that ■ silent majority that sits and waits for the master to put on his makeup and announce tomorrow's plan, they thrive on the fact that you are a dope-ridden, violent crew of bums. They fear everybody with long hair or a guitar; they fear all of you who are persecuted up and down this land for the smoking of an entirely harmless weed.

They try to tell you, the kinder ones, that this is a stage you'll grow out of and then you'll be just like them and life will go on. If you've got your ■, that should not happen. They try to tell you you're going to provoke the right wing and that you should remain quiet. Fuck the right wing. They try to tell you that it's more important if you want to take up with some of these causes that you get your degree, you go on to law school or medical school or dental school or accounting school, or wherever else you're going on to and then, Henry and Henrietta, you'll be in much better shape to promote your causes: as if these causes are some ladies' aid tea club or visiting an orphanage one day a month in order to expiate your own feeling of guilt. These are not causes that you take up and put down. This is the stuff of life and death. This is the way the world will run for as long as we can see in the future.

If these choices have been able to be made in the █ Republic, or the early days of the Third Reich, perhaps there wouldn't be all of those common, bulldozed graves. Perhaps if they could have had their thing together, if the Social Democrats and the Communist Party and the Jews, and the trade unionists would have kept together against a common enemy that was out to destroy them all, just as the common enemy is out to destroy us all, then perhaps they would not have achieved the only unity they ever were to achieve, that was the unity of death in those gas chambers. That type of unity has no meaning. It means nothing to anyone but the termites of the world.

The only meaning that has any real meaning to living people is the unity in life and that's what you have to maintain. You have an obligation to maintain that. You have an obligation to take the necessary steps to see that this war ends and doesn't end in a long period of attrition. Five and a half years of waiting have been marked by so many graves here and abroad, you have an obligation to stand and resist, not just to protest, but to resist and resistance means what it meant to the colonists.

I can imagine █ walking into Washington in 1772 and saying to the group of colonists as they sat around in somebody's living room, "Now you people can't go down to those ships in Boston Harbor and throw that tea in the water. That's violence. You just can't do that." Well, they did that after a period █ when they had tried everything under the sun to obtain a rational solution to a burning colonial problem. They didn't have the burning issues you have. That was a commercial revolution, the haves against the haves. They worried about tea taxes and stamp taxes, things that affected the wealthy rather than the poor. They couldn't even get the farmers to join in until they changed "life, liberty and property" to "life, liberty and the pursuit of happiness," which I guess is a euphemism for property, but those dumb farmers wouldn't know that.

You've got much more shining goals. You want a world of brotherhood. You want an end of war and racism and poverty. You want a type of life that has meaning to you, simply and personally to you. You want to go on to something which you think is enriching you and through your living, enriches other men and women. That is not something that you can call a lightly held goal or a commercial goal. You are the least commercial, thank God, generation in certainly my own lifetime. You want something fine and shining but you've got to be willing to fight for it. It's not something ■ by the mere asking and demanding. Now I don't know and I don't believe we're exactly at the Boston Tea Party ■ maybe we are, maybe we aren't. These are individual decisions that people have to make.

But I just want to end with one thought to all of you. We stood up here. I saw my wife put her fist in the air and I put my fist in the air. We're middle-aged people. This is not a gesture that comes normally to us. I feel awkward doing it. It's not my usual type of stance and eight months ago, before Chicago, I never did it. Chicago, in some mysterious fashion, taught me to put that fist in the air and that fist means resistance; it doesn't mean merely picketing, writing to your congressman or even electoral politics. It means resistance to illegitimate and immoral, indecent and unjust authority. So I implore you to keep it in the air. I hope someday you're able to open it and open it in the hand of brotherhood between all of us. And I hope you don't have to open it to curl that index finger around a rifle ■ but the possibility is there.

The gauntlet is down. ■ And I hope they will, fervently, but there is the possibility that they open [fire] in anger as I've indicated.

They have heard you but you must keep your voices loud and clear, because if they understand you and believe you, then maybe a miracle could happen and this country would change course, and with her the entire world [would] breathe a fervent sigh of relief and the killing and blood-letting and the oppression of the poor and the black and the Mexicans and the Indians, and all of the other ethnic and racial minorities that cry out so for some elemental justice, can end.

I hope the fist stays out. I hope it opens peaceably, but I recognize that the possibility is, that it may not. The choice is yours, Richard Nixon. I hope you hear us, as Marie Antoinette did not. Right on!

CHAPTER ELEVEN

DEFENDING FLAG BURNING AS SYMBOLIC SPEECH

EXCERPTS FROM KUNSTLER'S WINNING U.S. SUPREME COURT ARGUMENT DEFENDING THE BURNING OF THE AMERICAN FLAG AS A FORM OF PROTECTED SYMBOLIC SPEECH.

(*TEXAS V. JOHNSON,* 49 U.S. 397 (1989))

KUNSTLER: Mr. Chief Justice, may it please the Court.

Some of the steam has been taken out of me by some of the questions and some of the responses and the concession by the State. The State now apparently concedes that you can write out of the statute what Justice O'Connor referred to, the question of whether the actor knows or means that what he's doing will seriously offend one or more persons likely to observe or destroy [*sic*] or discover his particular act.

That's out of the statute, apparently, according to the argument, because in [both] the reply brief and today she has said essentially what is in the reply brief. Like Gertrude Stein, "A rose is a rose," they now say, "A flag burning is a flag burning." And they read out of the statute under which he was convicted and which went to the jury and the charge on the question of seriously offend, that's all out as far as Ms. Drew is concerned. But it's not out as far as this Court is concerned. That's what the conviction was about, that's what the argument to the jury was about, that's what the charge was about.

I think that what you have here is a statute that depends solely and exclusively on communicative impact on the audience, whether they're there or they read it in the newspaper or they see it on the screen in the evening.

[KUNSTLER RAISED TWO QUESTIONS: IS THE FLAG A SACRED SYMBOL? AND JUST WHAT IS A FLAG? —*ED.*]

KUNSTLER: And when you use the word "desecrate," you don't mean really in essence praising the flag. "Desecrate" has a meaning, and I just looked in Webster's Second International about it, and "desecrate" means "to divest of a sacred character or office; to divert from a sacred purpose; to violate the sanctity of; to profane; the opposite of consecrate."

It's used all over for commercial purposes. I notice that Barbara Bush wore a flag scarf, for example. There are flag bikinis, there are flag-everything. There are little cocktail flags that you put into a hot dog or meatball and then throw in the garbage pail. They're flags under the Texas Statute, something made out of cloth, but I think there are all sorts of flags used commercially. I'm not sure in my heart whether I think there's any control over the use of the flag, not on the criminal side anyway.

By the way, "national flag" does not just mean the American flag. There is a presidential flag – they don't put it in capitals – there is a presidential flag that is flown. The secretary of state has a flag that's a national flag. There are many national flags. I counted 17 national flags. Each department here in Washington has a flag. They're national flags, and the state of Texas would also include those as national flags, certainly the president's flag. So, I think that the word "national" flag needs definition in itself.

[UNDER SUPREME COURT PRECEDENT, SPEECH CANNOT BE PUNISHED UNLESS IT POSES A "CLEAR AND PRESENT DANGER" TO SOCIETY. KUNSTLER USED THIS PRECEDENT TO ATTACK THE TEXAS LAW. —*ED.*]

KUNSTLER: I think you must at least show some "clear and present danger," some imminence. The statute here is not limited to an imminent breach, by the way. It doesn't say imminent breach of the peace at all. It just says "likely" or "might" or "the actor could reasonably believe that someone might be seriously offended by it."

The Texas Court of Appeals treated this, I think, in its opinion. It said, "This statute is so broad that it may be used to punish protected conduct which has no propensity to result in breaches of the peace." Serious offense does not always result in a breach of the peace. The protest in this case did not lead to violence. And, I might add, in this protest they had policemen right along with them, undercover police officers. The crowd was not a large crowd. They estimate between 100 and 110, and Texas went on to say as with most other protests of this nature, police were present at the scene.

A witness was obviously seriously offended by the appellant's conduct because he gathered the burned flag and buried it at his home. Even though he was seriously offended, nevertheless he was not moved to violence. Serious offense occurred, but there was no breach of the peace, nor does the record reflect that the situation was potentially explosive. One cannot equate "serious offense" with "incitement to breach the peace."

[ANOTHER SUPREME COURT PRECEDENT — *WEST VIRGINIA V. BARNETTE* — RULED THAT SCHOOLS COULD NOT FORCE STUDENTS TO SALUTE THE FLAG. KUNSTLER DEBATED THE CASE WITH CHIEF JUSTICE REHNQUIST. —*ED.*]

KUNSTLER: With reference to the nationhood and national unity, which Ms. Drew raised and which is filled in in the brief, both the reply brief and the main brief of the State, I think – I thought *Barnette* set that to rest. I thought when Justice Jackson said that,

"If there is any fixed star in our constitutional constellation, it is that no official, high or petty, can prescribe what shall be orthodox in politics, nationalism..."

REHNQUIST: Well, the facts of *West Virginia v. Barnette* were quite different from this. There the students were required to salute the flag.

KUNSTLER: And here, Chief Justice, you're asking – people are required *not* to do something.

REHNQUIST: Yes.

KUNSTLER: And I think that's a comparable situation. We order you – we can't order you to salute the flag, we can't order you to do all these obeisances with reference to the flag. Can we order you not to do something to show something about the flag?

Can you say you can't force them to salute the flag or pledge allegiance to the flag, but can you then say we can force them *not* to show other means of disrespect for the flag, other means of protest over the flag by saying you can't burn the flag? I think they're the same, in all due deference. I don't know if I've convinced you, but...

REHNQUIST: Well, you may have convinced others. (*laughter*)

KUNSTLER: I would just like to end my argument – I think this is a fundamental First Amendment case, that the First Amendment to the written Constitution is in jeopardy by statutes like this. And I wanted to essentially close with two remarks. One, Justice Jackson said in *Barnette*,

> Those who begin coercive elimination of dissent soon find themselves eliminating dissenters. Compulsory unification of opinion achieves only the unanimity of the graveyard. The First Amendment was designed to avoid these ends by avoiding these beginnings.

And I think that's an important statement over the years from Justice Jackson.

And I understand that this flag has serious important meanings. The Chief [Justice] has mentioned many times that it's not just pieces of material, blue and white and red. That it has real meaning to real people out there. But that does not mean that it may not have different meanings to other people out there and that they may not under the First Amendment show their feelings by what Texas calls "desecration of a venerated object."

I think it's a most important case. I sense that it goes to the heart of the First Amendment. To hear things or to see things that we hate tests the First Amendment more than seeing or hearing things that we like. It wasn't designed for things we like. They never needed a First Amendment. This statute, or this amendment, was designed so that the things we hate can have a place in the marketplace of ideas and can have an area where protest can find itself. I submit that this Court should on whatever ground it feels right, should affirm the Texas Court of Criminal Appeals with reference to this statute and this conviction.

Thank you very much.

CHAPTER TWELVE

CONCERNING FREE SPEECH FOR RACISTS AND TOTALITARIANS

THIS SPEECH (CIRCA 1970) WAS FOUND AMONG KUNSTLER'S PAPERS. IT WAS WRITTEN TO BE DELIVERED AT A CONVENTION OF THE AMERICAN CIVIL LIBERTIES UNION (ACLU). IT IS NOT KNOWN IF THE SPEECH WAS EVER DELIVERED.

[THE ISSUE KUNSTLER ADDRESSED WAS WHETHER THE ACLU SHOULD REPRESENT AND DEVOTE ITS RESOURCES TO REPRESENTING NAZIS AND TOTALITARIANS. KUNSTLER BELIEVED IT SHOULD NOT. HE EVENTUALLY LEFT THE ORGANIZATION, EXPLAINING THAT HE CONSIDERED HIMSELF A MOVEMENT LAWYER AND THAT BY CONTRAST THE ACLU SAW THE CONSTITUTION AS ITS CLIENT, NOT THE MOVEMENT FOR SOCIAL CHANGE ITSELF. —*ED.*]

The basic issue posed by the syllabus is one over which there can (or should) be little significant disagreement among civil libertarians. Of course, the expression and dissemination of ideas, no matter how heinous, hateful, detestable, deplorable, banal or provocative, must be totally unfettered if the First Amendment is to have any real meaning. One does not even have to subscribe wholly to the absolutist views of a Black or a Douglass to support this concept of free speech in a society that professes to be an open one.

Some of the problems with which we are confronted here today stem, in large measure, from the Holmesian "clear and present danger" limitation created to meet, not a speech situation at all, but the inapposite "fire in a crowded theatre" analogy which obviously had nothing whatsoever to do with the communication of ideas, but rather with an irrational or malicious utterance and the dangerous panic likely to be caused by it. Unfortunately, this misleading phrase was soon in general constitutional usage as a means of inhibiting and even destroying freedom of expression. The instant a method of controlling a constitutional right is available for ready application, then the right affected by it is, to say the very least, in serious or deadly peril. Put more pertinently, when a factual determination of the potential or actual effect of the expression in question can prevent or punish its promulgation, then the concept of free speech is, in truth and in fact, a mythological one.

But the real question to be here debated is, to my mind, a political rather than a legal one. It simply cannot be adequately approached by the abstractions posed in the syllabus, namely whether:

1) "any limits may be placed on expressions of hate, advocacy of genocide or group libel";
2) "the freedom to speak includes the freedom to speak at times and places which are most offensive to listeners";
3) "the threat of violent reaction to speech justifies curbs";
4) "the expression of group hatred constitutes 'fighting words'"; and
5) "prior restraint [in view of the implications of 3) and 4)] is warranted."

If this panel is to have any real worth, it must come to earth somewhere so that the realities of the justification of the ACLU representation of American Nazis and the Ku Klux Klan can be adequately explored.

For me, the most pressing of those realities is the question of whether liberal and progressive organizations should in any manner support or represent the extreme right. I am familiar, as we all are, with most of the now routinized arguments regarding the wisdom of undertaking the Skokie case — they were summarized in the *New York Times* editorial last Sunday — and I find them intellectually satisfying and sound. But they are defensible only in the extreme abstract and do not take into consideration any of the concrete lessons of history.

If nothing else, we have, I hope, learned in this century the inescapable truism that the extreme right wing always tries first to destroy the left, and that it is the height of folly to believe that defending the liberties of the former will safeguard those of the latter. The Weimar Republic and Allende's Chile found that subscription to such a proposition was sadly and tragically misplaced. Such reliance is mistakenly grounded on the illusion of the acceptance of an existing body of law by every sector of the national community. Perhaps, because of this legalistic misconception, a sanguine appraisal of the power of the law to preserve human liberty has developed; a belief which has perpetuated the fantasy that supporting the bedrock rights of those who would destroy freedom is the surest way to preserve it.

If the Nazis, for example, subscribed to the same social contract presumably observed by the rest of us, then it might well be politic to take a chance on them. But we all know that this is simply not the case and, should they achieve power, they will quickly emulate their historical ancestors of the Third Reich and consume their enemies, real or imagined. The same can be said of the various Klans which likewise reject the universal applicability of constitutional liberties and guarantees, and can be expected, if ever in a position of authority, to withhold them from certain well-defined segments of the population.

Not a dependence upon law, but only the acquisition of a significant political base can protect the American left from those who would cheerfully destroy it. However, until such collective security becomes a viable reality, it is just far too dangerous to rely on a theory that has been consistently invalidated by history, *viz*, that the victorious struggle for the rights of would-be tyrants will insure those of their intended victims. The support of right-wing extremists by the ACLU through its attorneys is an act of such perilous self-deception that it is hardly compensated for by abstractional pipe dreams, or any favorable computations of pragmatic institutional gains over losses. It is wrong on every realistic (as well as moralistic) level and it should cease at once.

Instead, this organization, and every other one devoted to the preservation and extension of human rights, should be committing their limited resources solely and exclusively to the aid of those who do not categorically reject these goals. At a time when the country, aided and abetted by a repressive Supreme Court majority, is swinging perceptively to the right, (see, e.g., §§1302, 1328 and 1861, S.1437, passed by the Senate last January and presently pending as H.R. 6869 in the House of Representatives), those who would, had they but the power, further demolish the Bill of Rights insofar, initially, as Jews, Catholics and Third World people are concerned, cannot, in the name of decency, common sense and historical truth, be represented by progressive institutions and/or attorneys. The roads to hell may or may not be paved with good intentions, but those leading to the concentration camp and the lynching tree most certainly are not.

CHAPTER THIRTEEN

COMMEMORATING THE 1970 MURDER OF FOUR STUDENTS

THREE ANNIVERSARY SPEECHES AT KENT STATE UNIVERSITY IN KENT, OHIO.

KENT STATE*

The entry in Cambodia caused a shock,
Reverberating through the campus scene,
As long forgotten keys turned back the clock
And truth fell victim to a foul machine.

On Blanket Hill, a youthful khaki band
Watched silently as students made their vow
That to despoil another Third World land
Could not be tolerated by them now.

The guardsmen froze, their trigger fingers tense,
As M-1 rifles took a frightful toll
On those whose only crime was dissidence,
And four more victims joined the swelling roll.

In one young woman's anguished piercing scream,
The whole world heard the rupture of a dream.

---

*KUNSTLER WROTE THIS POEM ABOUT KENT STATE IN A COLLECTION OF SONNETS ENTITLED *TRIALS AND TRIBULATIONS*, GROVE PRESS (NEW YORK, 1985).

FIRST SPEECH, DELIVERED AT KENT STATE UNIVERSITY, MAY 4, 1988.

Thank you very much. I have come here many times before, five or six I think, in rain and in sunshine, in gymnasiums and out of gymnasiums. Tom only spoke of me,* but there were many lawyers and the latest ones tried desperately to stop the building of that gymnasium on Blanket Hill and to have Blanket Hill turned into a national monument, as it should be. We went to Federal Court in Cleveland. We had a sympathetic federal judge but he could not bend the law to force the government to make this a national monument.

And so we lost and when I left the Federal Courthouse in Cleveland, the judge said to me, "If I had it in my power," he said to [me], "I would grant the relief you wanted, but I don't."

But he said Blanket Hill should be a national monument. And so we came out of his chambers feeling [that] though while we had lost to the powers of darkness, we had at least shown one federal judge what the right path would have been.

Now a gymnasium covers part of that hill and it is a shame. There should be a monument there. It was a place where American patriots lived and died on May 4, 1970. It was a place where young blood was shed by people no older than themselves. It was a place of tragedy, and yet, out of it sprang a revulsion around this country that caused the closing of most of the institutions of higher

---

*WILLIAM KUNSTLER IS REFERRING TO TOM GRACE, WHO HAD JUST INTRODUCED HIM. HE HAD BEEN SHOT BY THE NATIONAL GUARD AT KENT STATE ON MAY 4, 1970.

education, that really brought an end to that ghastly war, if you can call it a war, in Southeast Asia.

The four who died here, the nine who were wounded here, the many who faced a Portage County Grand Jury and Petit Jury, they did more for their country than all the Nixons and the Agnews and the Reagans could possibly do. And they did it without consulting astrology or any other science. They did what they did because they believed in what they were doing. They learned the hard way what was happening to their brothers and sisters abroad, to themselves here and to their society. May 4 is a particularly memorable day in American history because 84 years to the day before May 4, 1970, there was another demonstration at the Haymarket Square in Chicago. And so similar to what happened here, because on May 3, 1886, strikers at the McCormick Harvester plant outside of Chicago had demonstrated. The mayor had called out the police. The police broke up the demonstration outside the Harvester works, killing one striker, wounding many others. And so, just as here, a demonstration was planned for the next day, the next evening at the Haymarket Square in Chicago.

At that demonstration a provocateur exploded a bomb. The bomb killed seven police officers and two members of the audience and wounded many others. And, as many of you know, the state of Illinois and the city of Chicago retaliated by trying eight of the demonstrators who were present at that rally, convicting them of murder and executing four of them by hanging at Joliet Prison. The remaining four were commuted by a true American, although he wasn't born here, John Peter Altgeld, who had the courage to jeopardize and eventually ruin his own career by commuting the death sentences of four of the eight. And as Clarence Darrow said at his funeral, "He freed the captives. He freed the captives."

So May 4 in the labor movement has always been an important date. And interestingly enough, the city of Chicago erected, on the site of the Haymarket explosion, a statue of a police officer with a commemorative sign in bronze, and I was happy to be present after May 4, 1970, to see students from the University of Chicago and elsewhere topple that sign as a sign of solidarity with another May 4 in their own lifetime.

Some of you here will remember that in 1977 we came back on May 4, and it was a bad day as far as the weather was concerned. It rained heavily and so we moved inside to Memorial Gymnasium, and on the platform sat two men, each in a wheel-chair. There was Ron Kovic, a Vietnam veteran who was paralyzed from the waist down after stepping on a mine in Vietnam. And there was Dean Kahler, a student of this university who was paralyzed for life by a National Guardsman's bullet. And toward the end of the services, Ron Kovic wheeled his wheelchair over to that of Dean Kahler, and these two men embraced each other then with tears rolling down their cheeks. And Ron Kovic said, and I will never forget the words, and there are people here who will remember them too, "Today at last Kent State and Vietnam are united as one."

It was a moment that I have never forgotten, and each year I hope that I am invited back because I relive it in my own mind. It is the stuff of which human emotions are made. Dean Kahler is not here today, and Ron Kovic is not here today, but if you close your eyes and think of two paralyzed young men in a wheelchair, one having his legs destroyed by a mine in that useless, senseless, immoral conflict in Southeast Asia and another having the same thing happen to him so many miles away on what should have been a peaceful American campus, and just visualize those two wheelchairs rolling toward each other and those two paralyzed human beings, paralyzed by the same war, the same conflict, embracing each other and saying, as it is true, Vietnam and Kent State are and were as one.

I would conclude with a sonnet that I wrote after Alan Canfora invited me to come here. I was sitting in a courtroom in New York going through the endless process of jury selection where I write all my sonnets. It saves your own sanity sometimes. You turn to other means of expression other than "objection" or "overruled" or what have you. The sonnet came out almost as if it had been written already in my brain, and I wanted to end with reading it to you.

A sonnet is a form of expression, a political form of expression that has been used since the early 17th century by writers in English, Italian, German and many other languages. And I decided to write sonnets after reading one by Edna St. Vincent Millay about the murders of Sacco and Vanzetti by the Massachusetts judicial system in 1927. This is called "Kent State Revisited."

Can it be true that it's been eighteen years
Since Blanket Hill soaked up the youthful blood
Of those whose only crimes were earnest tears
For each who had died in Southeast Asia mud?

They are united now who fell upon this hill
With all those who dropped ten thousand miles away
Destroyed by those they came so far to kill.
They never lived beyond the fourth of May.

Today they perish still around the world.
The guns have not forgotten how to speak
The flags of lunacy remain unfurled.
And earth yet does not comprehend the meek.

So now as then, impatiently we yearn
To know at last when will they ever learn.

Thank you.

SECOND SPEECH, DELIVERED AT KENT STATE UNIVERSITY, MAY 4, 1990.

Thank you very much. He was one young lawyer then. So was I, when all this happened. But he did mention the flag case and I just want to tell you that you have present in this room, you have Joey Johnson who was the defendant in the first flag case. He's somewhere right... There he is. He burned his flag in front of the Republican National Convention... in 1984 in Dallas. And with him is David Blaylock, who, last October after this second flag law was passed by the Federal Government, burned his flag on the steps of the Capitol to protest not only that flag law, but all the things the U.S. Government was doing domestically and abroad. Dave is a Vietnam vet and he is here, somewhere. Where is he? There he is!

That first two weeks in May of 1970 were two terrible weeks. As you know, the president invaded Cambodia, theoretically to search out sanctuaries for the Viet Cong in Cambodia. And shortly after what was called the Cambodian Incursion took place, there were demonstrations on many campuses, including this one. Now, May 4 occurred, this consonant tragedy, that we've been talking about today with speaker after speaker talking about it, in one way or another. And then, just 10 days later, at Jackson State, you had, in front of Alexander Hall, a barrage of bullets bored into that dormitory which took the lives of two young black men. I came to Kent State on May 5. We had a rally in the Kove, which I understand has been burned since then, but was then a meeting place in the town of Kent. It was wall-to-wall with people that came in to try to organize around what had happened the day before. We did organize a legal defense team. It included Ramsey Clark and many other people who came in [and] gave their services. We formed a Kent State Legal Defense Team, which proved to be extremely successful. And then when the hurt had barely begun to subside, the news of Jackson State came and I ran down to Jackson, Mississippi, where I gave, in another café or bar, I gave the same sort of speech I had given at Kent State and the same reaction occurred there. A legal defense team was organized, and the same emotions were parlayed into some sort of an organization against the authorities firing willy-nilly into a dormitory containing black students.

Some years ago in 1977, I came back here, and in the old gym we had a rally very much like this one. And it was a momentous rally for me. It was one I have never forgotten because on this stage were two men, both paralyzed by bullets in the spine. One was Ron Kovic, who received his bullet in Vietnam, and the other was Dean Kahler, who received his on Blanket Hill. Ron was the first one to speak and he wheeled his wheelchair up to the microphone [and] gave his speech. I can't remember a word of what he said in that speech. And then he wheeled back his wheelchair next to Dean's wheelchair, and then he reached over and put his arms around Dean and, in a voice that I will never forget, that tore the heat out of all of us in that room, he said, "Now Vietnam and Kent State are united forever." There wasn't a dry eye in the audience.

I wrote a sonnet about Kent State many years ago which I read, I believe, back in 1977. I wrote another one the other day which I will read to you before I continue these remarks. This is called "The Kent State Massacre – May 4th, 1970."

Just twenty years ago the shots rang out
That sent four students to an early grave

As youthful guardsmen filled with fear and doubt
Reacted to the orders of the navy.

The president decided to invade
Nearby Cambodia so he would know
By authoring such a lawless raid
It hit those sanctuaries full of holes.

On college campuses throughout the land
There were no classes open to attend
As strikers met morality's command
And vowed to bring the foray to an end.

The four who died were heroes, every one
Killed in the only war that must be won.

That is my feeling about what happened here. In the sonnet you'll notice I talk about "the orders of the navy," the governor of this state, Governor Rhodes at that time. There must be a special spot in hell for those people who are, in every sense of the word, murderers. And Governor Rhodes was a murderer. Chicky* may not be able to forgive the guardsmen who fired, but the real force behind that firing was the man who set the stage, created the climate and virtually induced that firing by his intemperate and irresponsible language. If there is anybody who should be doing time for those four murders, it is that man.

I hope, wherever he is, he hears these words and I hope that if there is a conscience left inside that brain, that that conscience begins to squirm. But sooner or later, if those who believe in the religious teachings of all religions and teach us that there is a place for people like that, then I hope that he is burning madly in wherever that particular hell that is preserved [*sic*] for him may exist. Even Dante would have a difficult time finding a place for him.

---

* KUNSTLER IS REFERRING TO ROSEANNE "CHIC" CANFORA, AN EYEWITNESS TO THE SHOOTINGS, WHO HAD MADE A SPEECH EARLIER IN THE PROGRAM.

These rallies are important because, in America, so many people do forget so quickly. They run to the tube. They run to spectator sports. And there probably is no coincidence that Super Bowls have Roman numerals because the Coliseum in Rome took the people's mind off what was happening down at the Forum.

Similarly, and not [to] forget, one writer talking about Watergate: William Safire, a former Nixon speech writer and a columnist for the *New York Times* now (maybe that's a step up or down, I'm not sure). But he said that he thought his countrymen and countrywomen would soon forget Watergate because, he said, "in this country, it's always darkest before the yawn." And it seems to me we can't let there be darkness before the yawn, that we have to keep remembering and never forgetting.

One reporter asked me, "Is this the time for reunion and forgiveness?" Maybe on some scores, but it's also time for remembering what Governor Rhodes and his minions did here and never forgetting what they did here and, in not forgetting, and in reminding the world, perhaps, maybe, we will keep it from happening again. It is only our memory that will do that, and our thoughts.

We must never forget what Frederick Douglass said, that you cannot have the ocean without the ocean's roar, that struggle must always continue, that there never is a time for green pastures or millennia, that the struggle to remain relatively free is a constant, ongoing effort and it must never stop. Our bodies must always be wherever that struggle [is]; and the moment we forget that, the moment we become lazy, the moment we sit back, then the evil ones do their ordained tasks to us.

The streets and the alleyways and the byways are our forums, and that's where we have to be if they try to reverse *Roe v. Wade* in the Supreme Court; if they try to bring back the back-door abortion clinics with the rusty hangers and all the rest; if they try to destroy our environment; if they try to kill blacks and Chicanos and Native Americans in the barrios and reservations and ghettos of this country; if they shoot down unarmed young people in the streets as they do in my city of New York on a regular basis. We have to react. Kent State is everywhere. It's in the back alleys of Harlem just as it was on Blanket Hill.

I would like to close and read the remarks of a Native American holy man, Black Elk. He watched in 1890, four days after Christmas, he watched the 7th Cavalry, an army of the United States, carrying the same flag that Joey Johnson burned (a few less stars perhaps), in Dallas, Texas, in 1984, and Dave Blaylock in 1989 on the steps of the Capitol, as [the soldiers] took out their Gatling guns and they mowed down 300 Sioux men and women and children, but mainly women and children who had been herded on to what was euphemistically called the Great Sioux Reservation. They shot down Big Foot and all of his 300 fellow Native Americans. Then after, they let them lie there for four days in a snow storm, shoveled the bodies into a common grave and Black Elk, a young man, watched this from a little hill out of range of the Gatling guns and he said the following:

> I did not know then how much was ended. When I look back now from this high hill in my old age, I can still see the butchered women and children lying heaped and all scattered along the river gulch, as plain as when I saw them with eyes still young. And I can see that something else died in the muddy blood and was buried in the blizzard. A people's dream died there. It was a beautiful dream. The nation's hoop is broken, scattered. There is no center any longer and the sacred tree is dead.

But he was wrong. The American Indian Movement proved that at Alcatraz and [at] the Bureau of Indian Affairs and back at Wounded Knee itself, the same site, in 1973. There is no ending to the hoop. The nation's hoop is not broken. There is a center. And the sacred tree is not dead so long as you are here and you are everywhere.

Thank you.

THIRD SPEECH, DELIVERED AT KENT STATE UNIVERSITY, MAY 4, 1992.

Normally I don't speak from notes, but I thought today was so important, particularly since it's a Monday and, as you all know, they died on a Monday here. And because it is the 22nd anniversary and, because our Kent family has grown over the years, we even include those who were not even born when those tragic events took place. So I felt I had to write down what I wanted to say so that it came out right, and it is dedicated to the entire Kent family, living and dead. And the entire family at Jackson State and some of the other places where people laid down their lives so that others might be free.

It is hard to believe that 22 long years have passed since the terrible events that took place on this campus, and which have been associated with it, in the eyes of the world, ever since. I arrived in Kent a day or so after the shootings and was privileged to be able to help to form the legal team that was eventually so successful in getting rid of the state prosecutions. I can still remember making a fiery speech to wall-to-wall students at the Kove on May 6, 1970. A Kove which is no longer there, which went up in flames some time later, with, I hope, no connection with my words.

As I look at the world today, I am reminded of that plaintive question in Pete Seeger's "Where Have All the Flowers Gone?", the song that seemed to characterize the utter futility of the so-called war in Vietnam in particular and all wars in general: "Oh, when will they ever learn, when will they ever learn?" Since the end of the Vietnam experience, our country has been engaged in tragic military involvement in such other Third World countries as Lebanon, Iraq, Panama, Grenada, Nicaragua, El Salvador, Peru, Chile and Honduras, to name but two handfuls.

On the domestic front, in one urban center after another, young blacks, Asians and Hispanics have been murdered in the streets by police officers who understand that they are carrying out the will of the dominant population. Even as we speak here, burnt-out buildings are still smoldering in South-Central Los Angeles and the ghettos of other cities, generated by outrageous acquittals in a case in which police brutality was so graphically recorded by a private citizen. Even today, a National Guard bullet has ended another young life in that benighted city. The Supreme Court, once the bastion of our most fundamental freedoms, is now engaged in a frenzied crusade to destroy the Bill of Rights, and to make sure that, as the only Western nation to sanction capital punishment, we kill those on death row as swiftly and as brutally as possible, whether they be innocent or guilty or were afforded due process of law. We have become the charnel house of the Western world.

At first blush, it seems that the young people who were shot down in the parking lot at the base of Blanket Hill gave up their lives for a dream that died with them. It's all too easy for many, in the 1990s, to regard the struggles of the past as aberrational and those living who participated in them as anachronisms. And yet we know, down deep in our hearts, that our comrades did not die in vain, that the pain of those whose bodies were torn by National Guard bullets was not uselessly endured, and that Arthur Hugh Clough was correct when he wrote, 130 years ago, in another time of international crisis:

Say not the struggle naught availeth,
The labor and the wounds in vain.
The enemy faints not, nor faileth,
And as things have been they remain.

For while the tired waves, vainly breaking
Seem here no painful inch to gain,
Comes silent flooding in, the main
Far back, through creeks and inlets making,

In from, the sun climbs slow, how slowly,
But westward, look, the land is bright.

Several years ago, author E.L. Doctorow delivered a most unusual commencement address at Brandeis University, in which he reminded his listeners that our country at the end of the 1970s and through the 1980s had lost much of the spirituality that was so evident in the day when Allison Krause, Sandy Scheuer, Jeff Miller and Bill Schroeder, and hundreds and thousands of America's finest young people, jeopardized their educations, their careers and even their lives to rise up and demand that their country live up to the promises of its professed principles. Mr. Doctorow ended his address with words that were as shocking as the truth sometimes is. As he put it:

> It's my view that in the last decade or so of life in our country... we have seen a national regression to the robber-baronial thinking of the 19th century. This amounts to nothing less than a deconstruction of America — the dismantling of enlightened social legislation that had begun to bring an equity over half a century to the lives of working people, to rectify some of the terrible imbalance of racial injustice and give a fair shake to the outsiders, the underdogs, the newcomers... We may have in fact broken down as a social contract in our time, as if we were not supposed to be a just nation, but a confederacy of stupid, murderous gluttons. So that, finally, our country itself, the virtue, the truth of America, is in danger of becoming a grotesque.

The 13 seconds that it took the members of Troop G of the 2nd Squadron, 107th Cavalry, of the Ohio National Guard to fire the bullets from their M-1 rifles that took four lives, crippled Dean Kahler for life, and wounded eight others, created a national revulsion against the incident itself and the tragedy of Vietnam that it personified. The closing of most of our colleges and universities generated by it was hard proof that the young people of this nation were not going to tolerate the indecencies perpetrated at home and abroad by the zealots in command. Although we didn't know it then, the die had been cast and it was only a question of time before our awful incursion into Southeast Asia would come to an end. For this, we owe eternal thanks to the restless shades of Allison, Jeff, Sandy and Bill, as well as the 56,000 of their contemporaries who surrendered their lives in the rice paddies and jungles of Vietnam.

Today, it is imperative that we, the living, rededicate ourselves to the eternal and endless struggle for peace, justice and freedom that has been waged, in one form or another, since humankind existed in organized societies. Like Herman Melville's great white whale, evil is perhaps as unconquerable as it must be unconquering. Ahab goes down, lashed to the huge mammal's back, the *Pequod* and all its crew are swallowed up in the raging sea, with one exception: Ishmael, the cabin boy, forever goes back to sea. In the words of the freedom fighters of Angola, Mozambique and Guinea Bissau, "*A luta continua.*"

Our victories may well be small ones, but we must fight for every possible beachhead, without hope of shortly arriving in green pastures but secure in the knowledge and belief that, only through constant and persistent resistance to the seemingly inexhaustible forces of oppression will we not only be able to hold back the night, but to advance our slow but steady march to a cleaner and a better day. This is perhaps what G.K. Chesterton had in his mind, in his poem, "The Vision of the King," when he has the Virgin Mary visit King Alfred, the Saxon monarch, on the night before the Battle of Athelny with the invading Danes, to inform him that, while he will surely be defeated on the morrow, the fight must go on.

I tell you naught for your comfort,
Yes, naught for your desire,
Save that the sky grows darker yet
And the sea rises ever higher.
Night shall be thrice night over you
And heaven and iron cope.
Do you have joy without cause
And faith without hope.

Incidentally, these words were the only ones published by *The London Times* on its editorial page the morning after the successful evacuation of the British and French armies from Dunkirk in the spring of 1940 so that they could live to fight another day.

Bernard Berenson, the great authority on Renaissance art, once described what Michelangelo must have had in mind when he carved his *David* out of a block of Carrera marble. The statue, he said, carried a message across the centuries, not simply of a fabled Biblical event, but of a young man on another hillside so long ago who pondered whether he dared to put the rock held loosely in his right hand into his sling and hurl it at the Philistine giant. Like Eliot's Prufrock, he must have wondered to himself, "Do I dare, do I dare?" In one way or another, these moments of potential jeopardy in pursuit of the ideal must come to us all, in one way or another, and the measure of our personal integrity is just how we respond to them. The four who died here and those who stood beside them on May 4, 1970, have fully and bravely responded to the central challenge of their time. May we all do the same for those of our era. If we do, they could have no finer memorial than this.

Some years ago, at another May 4, right on this campus, Ron Kovic, as I am sure many of you may remember, gave an enormously moving address about his own experience as a marine in Vietnam. When he finished, he pushed his wheelchair back alongside that of Dean Kahler, put his arms around him, and, in a voice

I shall never forget, screamed, "Now Vietnam and Kent State are forever united." As I prepare to sit down, I hope that all of you, whether you were present then or not, will keep that image in mind and vow that the answer to the eternal question, "When will they ever learn?" must be "some time" and not "never." The memories of all of our dead, civilian and military, as well as those in other countries slaughtered in our name, certainly deserve no less.

CHAPTER FOURTEEN

DEVOTING YOURSELF TO OTHERS

KUNSTLER WAS INVITED TO SPEAK ON A PANEL TO COMMEMORATE HIS YALE UNIVERSITY CLASS OF 1941. UNABLE TO ATTEND, HE SENT THESE REMARKS TO THE REUNION ORGANIZER.

When I was asked by Barry Zorthian to participate in the 35th Reunion program, I had many misgivings, not the least of which was a moral compunction against conducting a telephone conversation with a man who, according to my information, had played a significant role in carrying out our indecent and brutal policies in Vietnam. Although I promised to do so, I simply could not bring myself to call him back, but continued my discussions about the reunion with Frank Lavery instead. On second thoughts, however, I realize that my grievance is not with the Zorthians of this world, but rather against the system which creates and uses them for its own purposes.

I don't know whether I would have had the psychological fortitude to attend this or any other class reunion, but fate, in the form of the prosecution of four Native Americans for the alleged murders of two FBI agents on the Pine Ridge Indian Reservation last June, has provided me with a ready out. But, for some strange reason, I do want to communicate with people who, in the fall of 1937, started out with me as Yale freshmen. I am fairly certain that our goals then were relatively indistinguishable and that we all fervently longed to live the so-called American Dream which, in essence, meant the acquisition of material wealth, social status and acceptance, and as much power and influence in our areas of endeavor as would satisfy our individual psyches.

From my skimming of the *Alumni Magazine,* I know that many of you appear to have achieved these objectives in full measure. Yet I do wonder whether such outward success seems quite as desirable now as it did then and, if given the opportunity to start all over again, those who have achieved it would follow the same routes. But even as I write these words, I realize that they are as arrogant as they are pontifical and I will pursue them no further. I would rather devote my remarks to the thoughts of the only person for whom I can legitimately speak and that is myself.

It has taken me many years and much arduous introspection even to begin to understand the system in which we all live and my own relationship to it. Although my analysis is still far from complete, I have reached some conclusions which I want to share with you, in the hope that you will listen to me for a moment and accept at least the sincerity of what I am trying to say, no matter how strongly you may react to the thesis itself. If you will do this, then the hours which it has taken me to compose this whatever-it-is will have been unqualifiedly worthwhile.

As I have wandered the face of this country, going from one dreary courtroom to another, I have begun to realize that we are all lost in a well of human greed, in which spirituality, compassion and love are wholly alien concepts. Dominated by endemic racism and sexism, lured by the empty promises of material gain, and insisting on the unjustified prerogatives of birth and/or education, we have lost the ability to raise our eyes higher than our television screens. We are the elitist cogs of a civilization which measures human worth almost exclusively in terms of dollars and cents, and the fact that it has rewarded many of us handsomely, as it understands the meaning of that adverb, only underscores our real value to it.

In his novels, particularly *Heart of Darkness*, Joseph Conrad struggled to crystallize a comprehension of such a society. Yet even he, with all his powers of illuminating, by multicolored flares, the very darkness we would prefer to remain hidden, never fully exposed it at all. Perhaps the task is an impossible one, since the flaw is too grievous to be compatible with sanity. All we can do, I guess, is to be as honest as possible with ourselves and each other, and limit our once great expectations to the reality of the environment.

For me, in midlife, this effort has taken the form of engaging in perpetual struggle on rigidly restricted terrains for some aspect of relative freedom for others as well as for myself. I now know that these efforts will not result in the attainment of the millennium nor will they significantly affect the slow and tortuous progress of collective humanity. I have long since contented myself with the Melvillian concept of pursuing my vision of unconquering and unconquerable evil, painfully cognizant that the best any of us can do is to hold some portion of the field until we are better than we are. By such necessary limitation of objective, I have been able to survive as a person and function as the possessor of certain small but sometimes useful skills.

There is, naturally, some risk to such a course. But personal jeopardy is the *sine qua non* of true human progress. When I first saw Michelangelo's statue of David, I began to understand the real genius of the sculptor. Unlike all the other artistic portrayals of the future King of Israel, Michelangelo's version presents him in the moments *before* he had slain Goliath. He is shown with the rock in one hand and the sling in the other, at precisely the time he is deliberating whether to risk his neck or not. The personal war going on in his head as to whether he will dare or not is one with which we all have wrestled in one way or another, over the years of our lives. How we have resolved every such struggle is, in the main, known only to each of us, as the extent of personal risk, as well as the courage it evokes, can only be truly evaluated by the degree of privacy involved in its genesis.

I guess what I am trying to say, with as much earnestness as I can muster, is that the only life worth living is one which is devoted to the welfare of others. Everything else – the earning of daily bread, the satisfaction of individual ego, the attainment of personal goals – must remain avocation rather than vocation. Only then can the lasting nature of human interdependence be understood and affirmed. Or, as the mother of George Mead, the first, I believe, of our classmates to be killed in World War II, wrote to me after his death, "At least he died for, and not of, something."

If this be reason, make the most of it.

CHAPTER FIFTEEN

THE MOVEMENT IS NOT DEAD

THIS LETTER TO THE EDITOR OF THE *NEW YORK TIMES* WAS PUBLISHED ON MARCH 17, 1972. HERE, KUNSTLER REFUTES THE NEWSPAPER'S PERIODIC ASSERTIONS THAT "THE MOVEMENT IS DEAD."

To the Editor:

Several weeks ago I was interviewed in a Baltimore restaurant by one of your reporters who informed me that he was gathering material for what he characterized as a "mood piece." The result of this encounter appeared in your issue of February 21 under the unfortunate and highly misleading headline "Kunstler Agrees Left Is Less Militant."

While I have enormous respect and much affection for the reporter in question, I think that his article gives a totally false impression of both my opinions and my beliefs as to the state of the Movement for Social Change in America.

The Movement is not dead and can never die so long as there are men and women who continue to search for a cleaner, sweeter and more decent life, not only for themselves but for everyone everywhere. The Movement is not dead and can never die so long as there are some people, no matter how few, who search out horizons far wider than the restrictive boundaries of their own self-interest. The Movement is not dead and can never die until that day when not a single human being dares to step from safe obscurity and stand beside the hated, the feared and the despised.

As Fred Hampton so often used to say, "The beat goes on." In San José, Calif., Angela Davis is fighting for her life and those of her brothers and sisters in the life-denying ghettos and barrios of this paradoxical land of ours.

In Harrisburg, Pa., Philip Berrigan strides into court each weekday morning to give the lie to his country's calculated misuse of the judicial process. On college and university campuses across the land, young people have not lost their heartfelt conviction that we are better than we have become and that human love and comradeship are infinitely more desirable than the false security of a meaningless and hypocritical national mythology.

And D Yard at Attica now stands for the undeniable proposition that even barriers of steel and stone cannot blunt the endless quest of all mankind for some essential measure of dignity and worth.

To maintain one's perspective, it is crucial to recognize that all social movements, whatever degree of intensity they may once have had, must occasionally pause and regroup. But it would be the height of insensitivity to read into such hiatuses an end to high-blown ideals and the energy necessary to effectuate them.

That we are in such a period now, few would deny, but to over-magnify it into surrender and defeat is to misread all history and ignore the eternal incandescence of the human spirit. We wake even as we sleep and we live even as we die. The Movement is dead — long live the Movement!

William M. Kunstler
New York, March 17, 1972

AFTERWORD

BILL KUNSTLER, AN APPRECIATION

WILLIAM KUNSTLER DIED ON SEPTEMBER 4, 1995. THE HON. GUSTIN L. REICHBACH WROTE THIS APPRECIATION OF HIM IN THE *NEW YORK LAW JOURNAL* ON NOVEMBER 13, 1995. JUDGE REICHBACH SITS ON THE SUPREME COURT IN BROOKLYN, NEW YORK.

The 1960s witnessed the start of an enormous expansion of the legal profession. It was the dawn of an era when many, myself included, were drawn to the profession not for its traditional lures of prestige and fortune but rather out of a commitment to the dispossessed and opposition to the forces of domination. As a young boy I had read *Attorney for the Damned,* a collection of Clarence Darrow's most famous courtroom summations.

Darrow was my hero and inspiration. Labor's greatest champion, Darrow traveled the country, transfixing juries as he represented the militant heroes of the nascent workers' movement under attack by both the state and armed corporate might. Defending union president William Kidd in Wisconsin, Eugene Debs in Chicago, or "Wobbly" leader "Big Bill" Haywood in Idaho, Darrow was the circuit-riding champion of the despised and feared. While reviled at the time as an advocate of violent revolution and defender of anarchists and terrorists, today Clarence Darrow is hailed as the very symbol of courage and conscience.

If Darrow, the "attorney for the damned," was the first half of this century's greatest champion of the disadvantaged and vilified, William Kunstler will, in the fullness of time, undoubtedly occupy a similar singular position in the history of the second half of the 20th century. Indeed, while the parallels are striking, a fair appraisal suggests that Kunstler's victories were won over considerably more varied legal terrain and were of far greater lasting constitutional impact than Darrow's.

The careers of both had conventional beginnings. Darrow served as Chicago's corporation counsel, then became general counsel for the Chicago & Northwestern Railroad. In 1894 Eugene Debs led the American Railway Union on strike and Darrow resigned to represent Debs against federal criminal conspiracy charges, beginning his career as a people's lawyer.

Bill Kunstler began practising law with his brother in the early 1950s, building a modestly successful civil practise. In the early 1960s he began making roaming forays across the Deep South, representing Martin Luther King, Jr., Freedom Riders and the leaders of the Student Nonviolent Coordinating Committee.

The turning point in Darrow's career, after a decade of representing union leaders, came in 1907 when he successfully defended IWW leader "Big Bill" Haywood, charged with the assassination of the ex-governor of Idaho. Darrow, to the horror of his respectable admirers, declared his unqualified loyalty to his clients in their battle against capital, declaring to the jury, "I don't care how many wrongs they committed... how many crimes... how many brutalities they are guilty of. I know their cause is just."

Kunstler, like Darrow, was assailed for supporting and identifying too closely with his clients and their cause. For Kunstler, after a decade of success in civil rights cases, the transforming event was his involvement in the Chicago Conspiracy Trial in 1970. From that moment Kunstler made an irrevocable commitment on behalf of the dispossessed and in opposition to the forces of power and privilege. Thereafter, Kunstler chose to unconditionally support people of color, the weak, the scorned, the embattled, the unpopular.

Darrow's singular constitutional case was the Scopes "monkey trial" in 1925 in Tennessee, where he appeared on behalf of the American Civil Liberties Union to attack that state's prohibition on teaching evolution. As an appellate counsel, Kunstler's advocacy spanned three decades, beginning with numerous U.S. Supreme Court victories during the civil rights era. In 1984 Kunstler successfully argued the unconstitutionality of New York's death penalty law. In 1989 he prevailed before a conservative Supreme Court which upheld his claim that flag-burning was protected First Amendment activity. The Scopes case was the only one in Darrow's career in which he appeared without fee. For Kunstler, after Chicago, the retained case was [the] exception in his massive caseload.

Near the end of both their careers Darrow and Kunstler were attacked by former allies, accused of selling out. In Darrow's case the charge was wealth; in Kunstler's, fame. Darrow was 67 when he defended Leopold and Loeb, sons of Chicago's wealthiest families, in a brutal "thrill" killing case. Kunstler at 70 was similarly assailed for appearing on behalf of John Gotti, the "Teflon Don." Despite the criticism, both men took on these cases because they implicated long-standing principles each held dear. For Darrow, it was his opportunity to argue against capital punishment; for Kunstler, a chance to vindicate the principle that the government could not deny a defendant [the] counsel of their choice.

On Labor Day 1995, William Moses Kunstler, America's most controversial lawyer, died at the age of 76. For more than three decades, Bill was a legal bulwark and ever-available zealous defender of the social change movements that have shaped our times. Many were surprised to learn Bill was 76, he seemed both so ever-present and so ageless. Kunstler, learning from clients like Abbie

Hoffman, reveled in his notoriety and masterfully used the attendant public attention he could command to benefit his client's case and cause. Yet Bill's celebrity tends to overshadow the enormous range of his advocacy skills. At a time when the legal profession is increasingly narrowly specialized, Bill Kunstler's range of achievements included unlikely acquittals in seemingly hopeless criminal trials, civil litigator and master of procedural strategy and appellate advocate including constitutional appeals in the U.S. Supreme Court and the highest courts in many states.

Critics tried to deprecate Bill's legal skills and, ignoring his tremendous rapport with jurors, accused him of "grandstanding," calling him "reckless" and a publicity hound. Bill's record of trial victories in seemingly impossible circumstances is easily the equal of the dazzling successes of the great Darrow. In the 1970s, in the hostile environment of the Midwest, Bill won an acquittal of American Indian Movement militants charged with murdering an FBI agent. His "reckless" charges of FBI misconduct were later substantiated by the trial judge. In the 1980s, Bill won acquittal of Larry Davis by "recklessly" claiming that the police were enmeshed in a web of drug corruption. Years later, precincts in Harlem and the South Bronx witnessed dozens of officers taken out in handcuffs. Bill Kunstler was occasionally reckless, arrogant, silly, headstrong, and Bill Kunstler's instincts were invariably right.

Beyond his trial work, Bill could be an innovative legal thinker. In the early 1960s, at a critical junction in the anti-apartheid struggle in this country, when the momentum of the Southern civil rights movement was threatened by mass arrests and summary convictions and sentences in racist local courts, Bill and his Lawyers Guild colleague, Professor Arthur Kinoy, discovered and employed an unused statute from the Reconstruction era to remove those local prosecutions to the federal courts and thus keep demonstrators on the street.

Living Oliver Wendell Holmes's admonition to "share the action and passion of his time," Kunstler inspired three generations of socially committed lawyers by the simple example of his life — the obvious delight he took in his battles against the high and mighty. Bill was deeply trusted by the most remarkable range of people who, finding themselves blinded by the glare of sudden notoriety, knew they could depend on him to unstintingly champion their interests. But remarkably, Bill was also there in hundreds of nonfamous cases bringing the same enthusiasm and commitment to the people he represented.

Bill had a grand time and showed the possibility that the unceasing quest for justice could be a joyous one. Beyond his brilliant lawyering and bravura personality, Bill was a cultured intellect and man of letters. He earned a Yale B.A. in French, a law degree from Columbia and was the author of legal texts, popular histories and volumes of verse. I last saw him at the National Arts Club, reading his sonnets. While Bill would no doubt prefer a snippet of his own verse, I am confident he would be pleased with these lines from "Satisfaction" by lawyer, beloved national poet and Guatemalan revolutionary, René Castillo, who before his execution by the Guatemalan Army in 1967 wrote:

The most beautiful
for those who have fought a whole life
is to come to the end and say:
We believed in people and life,
and life and the people
never let us down.

And so they are won for the people
And so the infinite example is born.
Not because they fought a part of their lives
but because they fought all the days of all their lives.

And so they are, distant fires,
living, creating the heart
of example.

CONTRIBUTORS

Michael Steven Smith and Karin Kunstler Goldman practise law in New York City. With co-editor Michael Ratner, they also edited *Politics on Trial: Five Famous Trials of the 20th Century*, by William M. Kunstler (Ocean Press).

Sarah Kunstler is a law student at Columbia Law School. She and Karin are two of William M. Kunstler's daughters.

Michael Ratner is the President of the Center for Constitutional Rights (New York) which is representing prisoners held in the U.S. base at Guantánamo Bay, on occupied Cuban territory.

ALSO FROM OCEAN PRESS

COVERT ACTION

THE ROOTS OF TERRORISM

Edited by Ellen Ray and William H. Schaap

"The essays in this collection could hardly be more timely, or more informative, and cannot be ignored by those who hope to gain a serious understanding of what is unfolding today."
—Noam Chomsky

Key articles from the authoritative magazine *CovertAction*, presenting a comprehensive background to the terrorist attacks of September 11, 2001, and the current "war on terrorism." Contributors include Noam Chomsky, Eqbal Ahmad, Edward Herman, Philip Agee, and many others.

310pp, ISBN 1-876175-84-2 (paper)

BIOTERROR

MANUFACTURING WARS THE AMERICAN WAY

Edited by Ellen Ray and William H. Schaap

"*Bioterror* is a valuable antidote to the view that the United States opposes chemical and biological warfare. This book shows in detail how this country has been a pioneer in both the development and use of chemical-biological weapons." —Edward S. Herman

100pp, ISBN 1-876175-64-8 (paper)

WARS OF THE 21ST CENTURY

NEW THREATS, NEW FEARS

Ignacio Ramonet

An activist intellectual like Noam Chomsky, Ignacio Ramonet is the internationally recognized and respected editor of the prestigious *Le Monde diplomatique* (published monthly with the *Guardian* newspaper from Britain). For the first time this articulate and radical voice is presented to English-language readers, discussing the fundamental global issues at stake in the recent wars in Iraq, Afghanistan, Kosovo and elsewhere.

200pp, ISBN 1-876175-96-6 (paper)

ALSO FROM OCEAN PRESS

radical history

CHILE: THE OTHER SEPTEMBER 11

Edited by Pilar Aguilera and Ricardo Fredes

An anthology that reclaims the day of September 11 as the anniversary of the U.S.-backed coup in Chile in 1973 by General Augusto Pinochet against the popularly elected government of Salvador Allende.

80pp, ISBN 1-876175-50-8 (paper)

Published in Spanish by Ocean Press as *Chile: El Otro 11 de Septiembre* (ISBN 1-876175-72-9)

ONE HUNDRED RED HOT YEARS

BIG MOMENTS OF THE 20TH CENTURY

Edited by Deborah Shnookal

Preface by Eduardo Galeano

"It's the adventure of making changes and changing ourselves which makes worthwhile this flicker in the history of the universe that we are, this fleeting warmth between two glaciers." —Eduardo Galeano

80pp, ISBN 1-876175-48-6 (paper)

GUANTÁNAMO

A CRITICAL HISTORY OF THE U.S. BASE IN CUBA

David Deutschmann and Roger Ricardo

A comprehensive and timely analysis of the controversial U.S. naval base in Cuba. This expanded edition discusses the legal and the political implications of the continued U.S. occupation of Cuban territory and the indefinite detention of "enemy combatants" captured in the "war on terror."

100pp, ISBN 1-920888-04-7 (paper)